A Documented Modern-day Miracle

GOD'S
Strategy
for
Tragedy

BEN GODWIN

Ben Godwin
P.O. Box 3161• Jasper, AL 35502
(205) 686-5478
Website: www.bengodwin.org

Publisher's Cataloging-in-Publication
(Provided by Quality Books, Inc.)

Godwin, Ben.
    God's strategy for tragedy : a documented modern day miracle / Ben Godwin.
    p. cm.
    Includes bibliographical references.
    LCCN 2008923438
    ISBN-13: 978-0-942507-45-4
    ISBN-10: 0-942507-45-2

    1. Godwin, Ben. 2. Spiritual healing—United States. 3. Clergy—United States—Biography. 4. Christian biography—United States.   I. Title.

BT732.5.G63 2008   248.8'9'092
                          QBI08-600105

God's Strategy For Tragedy
Copyright © 2008 Ben Godwin

Cover art by Keith Morris. Cover layout and design by Lonzo Kirkland.

Printed in the United States of America

Published by **Deeper Revelation Books**
P.O. Box 4260 • Cleveland, TN 37320-4260
Phone: 423-478-2843 • Fax: 423-479-2980
Website: www.deeperrevelationbooks.org
Revealing "the deep things of God" (1 Cor. 2:10)

Wholesalers and bookstores should direct orders to:
Deeper Revelation Books

Ben Godwin

Ben's third grade photo, at age 8, taken shortly after he received his miracle in the fall of 1977.

Dedication

Bertha Madden was my pastor for the first seventeen years of my life. She dedicated me as an infant and was present for my baptism when I was a lad. Her compassion for me in prayer when I needed a miracle paved the way for the testimony contained in this book. She, along with my parents, recognized the call of God on my life to preach when I was eight years old.

Sister Madden was truly a prophetess of the Lord. She started a prayer meeting in her home in 1957 that blossomed into a thriving church. Her primary ministry was intercessory prayer. She hosted Thursday morning and Friday night prayer meetings in her home faithfully for nearly thirty years. Besides pastoring our church, *The House of Hope*, she wrote a book of inspirational poetry entitled, *Bound To Bless*. She was also an excellent Bible teacher and published numerous Gospel tracks and articles. Her teaching and prayer ministry literally touched people from all over the world.

Sister Madden had confidence in me and gave me the opportunity to preach from her pulpit at the age of thirteen. Thereafter, she entrusted me with one Sunday night service per month for four years to develop my ministry gifts. She coached me along with gentle instruction and loving correction mixed with steady doses of encouragement. She even wrote a poem to compliment my high school graduation speech. She believed in me; therefore, I believed in myself.

She was a mighty prayer warrior and a precious family friend. Bertha Madden went home to meet her Savior and receive her reward on March 1, 1990, at the age of ninety-two.

Foreword

Ben Godwin, the young man sharing the story of his miracle leg, has been rightfully termed as a "physical and spiritual phenomenon!" With the touch of God's hand on Ben's leg, there came an accompanying touch on his life that has been an even greater miracle.

At the age of thirteen, stretching his "new limb" to enable him to be seen above the pulpit, little Ben preached what was his first sermon. Since then, he has continued to lift up the name of the Lord who healed and called him into the ministry. Years of preparation and continuous preaching have included many churches, schools and youth gatherings in numerous states and cities. Accompanying gifts accredited are Ben's writings and musical ability. With his continued life-style of discipline, dedication and humility, we believe Ben to be well on his way to becoming one of God's elect for the purpose of "Preparation preaching for the end time days."

I am among those who prayerfully watch the progress of this one dedicated before birth and reared in a Christian home. My expectation of him is a miracle walk, on a miracle leg, in a miracle ministry...a life fulfilled and a glory to God.

– *Bertha Madden* (Ben's late pastor)

Acknowledgments

Leslie and Sylvia Godwin as known to others, but they are Mom and Dad to me. I greatly appreciate and honor them for the time, work and love they diligently invested into my life. Being raised in a stable, godly home is an irreplaceable heritage that I cherish. I am grateful for the sacrifices they made to educate me in Christian schools. They have always been my most avid supporters as I have pursued the will of God for my life. As they face their golden years, I trust the direction of my life will always be a source of joy to them. I only hope they are as proud of me as I am of them.

I am forever indebted to Evangelist Mike Shreve, my mentor and spiritual father, for his guidance, example, and loyalty. He gave me unimaginable opportunities in ministry for which I will always be grateful. Every success I achieve in ministry is largely due to his influence.

I am especially thankful for my wife, Michelle. She is my true love, best friend and the greatest gift that God has given me, second only to salvation. Her support and encouragement in all my ministry endeavors is a constant source of inspiration. Her pure heart and faithful spirit is "the wind beneath my wings." I also thank God for my three precious children, Nathan, Emily and Noah. Every day they produce lasting memories to cherish. I pray that I can be to them the type of role model and father that I was fortunate to have.

Finally, I want to thank Bunny Bateman for the typesetting and layout of this manuscript. I also want to thank the proofreaders—Winnie Shreve, Jeanne Obee, and Gary Pollard, for their assistance in finalizing this book for the press.

-Ben Godwin

Table of Contents

Danger Ahead

There was no time to think or react. All I could do was watch helplessly as the car slammed into me and my bicycle.

As the bike was dragged under the car, an invisible hand guided my slender frame safely to the hood. When the car skidded to a halt, I tumbled violently to the ground. Dazed, I didn't feel any pain. In fact, I didn't even notice the blood that had soaked my left sock and pant leg. Slowly, I tried to stand up, thinking I had escaped injury. I was wrong. My left leg collapsed underneath me. Lying there on the road trembling, I suddenly wished I was home. Little did I know it would take **three weeks** to get there.

Every once in a while something happens that reminds us how fragile life really is. In a split second, everything we think we are entitled to can be stripped away like shingles in a hurricane. July 16, 1977, began as a routine summer Saturday, but the course of my life was drastically altered by the events of that day.

A Godly Heritage

I grew up in a suburb of Tampa, Florida, called Carrollwood. Our family lived in a four-bedroom, brick house situated on six acres of lake-front property. Our land was home to a one hundred tree orange grove that attracted seasonal Northerners who "migrated" to Florida's warm climate for the winter. I found it amazing how many "snowbirds" stopped by our little grove to pick their very first orange.

To this day, after being reared on fresh-squeezed citrus, I cringe at the thought of store-bought, concentrate juices. Just call me spoiled! Every year during the holidays, we would pick several bushels of fruit and give them to friends, neighbors, fellow church members, my dad's employees or nursing home patients. Our orange orchard also made the perfect arena for numerous rotten orange fights between me and my brothers and the neighborhood kids.

The Godwin family lived comfortably thanks to my father's prosperous company, Builder's Hardware, Inc. He built it from scratch and kept on scratching until it mushroomed from our garage into an 80,000 square foot warehouse, with over sixty employees and fifteen delivery trucks. My mother deliberately chose not to pursue a secular career. Instead, she was a devoted house-wife, no less a full-time job. In all, my folks raised six kids: four boys (Kenny, Joel, Jesse and me) and two girls (Cindy and Janna). Mom affectionately calls our family a "boy sandwich" because the boys were born "sandwiched" between the two girls. Cindy is the firstborn and Janna is the caboose on the Godwin train. Occasionally, Mom dotes about having four sons with "bookend" daughters.

We were blessed to be raised in a stable, Christian home. My parent's visible love for each other and love for us was a cohesive factor that carried us through the tough times. Attending church and family devotions were as much a part of our lives as swimming, fishing and water skiing in the lake behind our house. My father led me to the Lord during family devotions one night when I was only six. I fondly remember kneeling down on my knees at the couch in our living room, praying the sinner's prayer and asking Jesus to come into my heart. Shortly thereafter, my dad, who was an elder and an ordained minister in our church, baptized me in our lake. (Our church didn't have a baptistery, so all of our baptismal services were conducted at the Big Bay Lake.) Ironically, I have experienced the same privilege of baptizing my own son, Nathan, and daughter, Emily. As a boy I grew up knowing right from wrong and my childhood was very happy, normal and, to me, ideal.

Childhood Mischief

All six of us kids got into our share of mischief. Jesse once accidentally drank gasoline as a kid. He turned blue and began gasping for air. But when Mom and Pastor Madden prayed for him, he recovered with no ill effects. Joel once got stuck in our garage door. It had a primitive automatic opener on it. Sometimes, if an airplane flew over too close, we would come home to find the door wide open. Joel pushed the open/close button and tried to see how many times he could roll under the door before it came all the way down. Predictably, the door came down on his back and pinned him to the ground. There he stayed kicking and screaming until our babysitter freed him.

My baby sister, Janna, had a unique prayer answered as a toddler. She asked Mom to buy her a rabbit. Rather than go to a pet store, Mom decided to pray with Janna for a pet rabbit. A few days later my dad was mowing in our orange grove and "coincidentally" flushed out a whole rabbit family from some brush. We caught two of the babies and Janna had her prayer answer. Unfortunately, she tried out her veterinary skills on them and, unaware of the hazard, doused them with motor oil. They both died and Janna was devastated.

Even our family dog, Rascal, a collie, sniffed his way into trouble. Once he was bitten by a large rattlesnake and trotted into our carport with blood dripping off his nose. As crazy as it sounds, my parents laid hands on him and prayed. (After all, the Bible says, "Preach the Gospel to every **creature**" doesn't it?) A veterinarian later estimated by the spread of the fang marks that the snake was between six and eight feet long. To our amazement, Rascal's nose didn't even swell and he lived for several more years.

There was one stunt I pulled that my brothers and sisters will never let me live down. One night when I was a toddler, I took all of the presents under our Christmas tree to my room and unwrapped every single gift. My mother discovered me sound asleep in a heap of wrapping paper the next morning. My mom and my sister, Cindy, had to rewrap every gift. My perfectly logical explanation is that I was simply doing what the Bible says, "Neglecting not the gifts." As you can see, we had lots of fun and excitement

> *I was simply doing what the Bible says,*
> *"Neglecting not the gifts."*

as kids. We produced many fond memories too numerous to recount. Our family is still very close-knit in spirit even though we are spread out in five different states.

As a typical large family, we had many incidents and mishaps but nothing life-threatening. In fact, until my accident, none of us had even broken a bone. That is truly remarkable when you consider how many tree forts we built, basketball and football games we played, tractors and boats we drove and how many bicycles and roller skates we wore out.

By the time my older brothers reached junior high school, they began dabbling in things that were taboo in our house (i.e., rock-n-roll music, smoking cigarettes and marijuana, drinking beer, etc.). Often I would spy on them and catch them smoking. Naturally, being an impressionable kid, I wanted to be "cool" like them, so I began stealing cigarettes and taking an occasional puff. I learned from my sly brothers to cover the smoky smell on my fingers by rubbing green leaves between them. Whenever we went into the house after a smoke, we made a bee-line for the bathroom to freshen our breath with mouthwash.

Concealing the evidence was crucial. If or when my parents discovered our devious habits, we knew what to expect—Daddy's feared belt for starters, our mouths washed out with soap (my mom's specialty in cases of cursing or other sins of the mouth), being grounded for sure and writing "I will never smoke again" on a piece of paper one hundred times. You see, when my parents disciplined us they were patriotic—they gave us stripes and we saw stars!

Lest you get the wrong impression, let me clarify and emphasize that my parents were not abusive or overbearing. They believed in the old-fashioned, Biblical, spare-the-rod-spoil-the-child disciplinary approach that is desperately lacking in today's society. We were given lots of freedom to be kids and there was no undue pressure on us to grow up prematurely. But if we crossed over certain behavioral boundaries, we knew to beware. Two things were crystal clear in our household: our parents loved us unconditionally and true love doesn't allow someone to persist in self-destructive behavior.

Riding Into Trouble

As previously mentioned, July 16, 1977, began as a typical Saturday. My brothers and I worked up a sweat mowing grass and doing other chores. Then we went for a refreshing dip in our lake. There they nominated me to ride to a nearby service station to buy some cigarettes for us to share. They were keeping a low profile after being caught and grounded by my parents for smoking. They knew our parents would least suspect me, an "innocent" seven year old.

Leaving my brothers at the lake, I ran to our house to change clothes and get money. With dripping shorts and a troubled conscience, I entered the back door. Voices echoed from the living room. (My parents had a lawyer and his wife over to discuss business.) Tip-toeing across the kitchen floor, my heart pounded in my chest like a bass drum. My eyes darted nervously as I peered around the corner to survey the long hall. Quickly, I scurried past the conference, down the hall and into our bedroom.

Once inside, I changed from my soaked swimsuit into a pair of jeans, a T-shirt, and my green Converse All Star tennis shoes. Grabbing a handful of coins from the top of the dresser, I stuffed them into my pocket and bounded down the hall and out the front door, deliberately avoiding eye contact with Mom and Dad.

In the carport, I rolled up my right pant leg so it wouldn't get caught in the chain on my brother's ten speed. His bike was much too big for me and, to make matters worse, he had removed the brakes, a popular fad of that time. (He invented a custom braking method: whenever he wanted to stop, he swung either leg back behind him and held his shoe against the rear tire. The friction caused by the "brake shoe" gradually brought the bike to a halt. Ingenuity, huh? And our parents wondered why our shoes wore out so quickly.)

Hopping on this unroadworthy contraption, I sped out of the driveway, hardly noticing it was beginning to drizzle. With over a mile to go, I pedaled vigorously. During the ride I kept wondering if I would get caught and be punished. Pelted by raindrops, I pushed my troubled thoughts aside and continued my journey. Rain blurred my vision. Mud spun off the rear tire causing my shirt to stick to my back. Steam floated off the hot pavement. But I kept riding—straight into the hungry mouth of trouble.

Finally, I made a right turn onto Stall Road. The Texaco service station was just ahead. (How swiftly my feet were running into mischief!) I pulled into the station, out of breath. Getting off the bike, I laid it against the curb and walked inside. A quick glance through the office found it empty. I could hear the attendant talking with the mechanic out in the garage. Quickly, I pulled the change out of my pocket and shoved sixty-five cents into the vending machine (cigarettes were cheap back then). When the coins registered, I yanked on the lever and the package dropped to the tray below. I walked over to the counter, picked up a book of complimentary matches and dashed outside, around the corner and into the restroom to stash the contraband in my pants. I walked out, picked up my bike and started home. Nineteen days later I finally made it there.

> *I walked out, picked up my bike and started home. Nineteen days later I finally made it there.*

Oblivious to danger, I rode right into the path of an oncoming car. It was still sprinkling and a bush obstructed my view. I didn't see the car coming until it was too late. The horn blew and the car skidded toward me on the wet asphalt. Helplessly, I watched the bumper of the car (traveling approximately 30 m.p.h.) collide with me and the bike. The bike was crushed underneath the car. Fortunately, I flipped on top of the hood. When the car came to a screeching halt, the forward momentum threw me to the pavement. It happened so fast that I didn't feel any pain.

Dazed, I couldn't tell if I was injured. I slowly struggled to my knees and propped myself up on my right leg. But when I stood and put weight on my left leg, it compressed together like an accordion and collapsed underneath me. I was unaware that a three inch piece of my shinbone (the Tibia, large lower leg bone) was lying on the road. When the car rammed into my left leg,

I suffered two compound fractures. The impact literally knocked a chunk of bone out the other side, leaving a six-inch gaping wound. Three inches of bone was completely dislodged from my leg. The Fibula (the small lower leg bone) was also broken and penetrated through the top of my shin. All of this damage was hidden beneath my bloodied jeans.

Within moments, a curious crowd of onlookers gathered. They urged me to remain still on the ground. Some just stared in horror. Someone asked for my parent's names, my address and phone number. Amazingly, I was alert enough to relay the information. One of the first people to reach the scene was a doctor who "just happened" to be passing by. (Coincidence, you know, is when God orchestrates events and remains anonymous.) I'm convinced the Lord led him there because he knew exactly how to treat my leg until the paramedics arrived.

At this point my story may seem like one of the thousands of unfortunate accidents that occur every day. As this testimony unfolds, however, you will see that this case is unique. You will see the sovereign hand of God at work in many of the details. While God certainly did not cause this accident, I do believe He allowed it in order to serve a higher purpose.

Even at age seven, rebellion in its spawning stages had seized my rapidly hardening heart. (The human heart is like wax—place it near heat and it softens, take it away from the heat and it hardens.) I was drifting in a dangerous direction spiritually, away from the fire of God's love. The fact that I was raised in a Christ-centered home and even attending Christian school was no guarantee that I would automatically live for God. I was a free moral agent. I had the freedom, as everyone does, to make my own choices. This accident was truly a blessing in disguise because it made me re-evaluate my life's direction.

Unfortunately, it often takes drastic measures for God to get people's attention. In the long run, it's worth whatever it takes to make it to heaven. Jesus taught that it is better to enter heaven handicapped than to be healthy and end up in hell (Mt. 5:29–30). We will discuss in later chapters how God can use tragedy to draw people closer to Himself. Suffice it to say that God can bring good out of any bad situation. I am living proof of that truth.

A Perilous Plot

The paramedics arrived in a matter of minutes. The doctor at the scene explained to them the extent of my injuries. An Emergency Medical Technician (EMT) removed my blood-soaked sock and shoe and cut the seam of my left pant leg from the hem to the knee. Then they carefully placed an air cast on my leg which served to restrict movement and prevent infection. By this time my horrified parents drove up. They had been praying from the moment they were phoned with the distressing news. I know it came as a devastating shock to them. They didn't even know I had left our property, much less traveled a mile and a half away without their permission. My dad loaded my brother's "critically injured" bicycle into the back of our station wagon.

Incidentally, I can only imagine the extent of my injuries had I ridden my own bike that day. My bicycle was much shorter than my brother's ten speed. The car would have struck me much higher—probably around the chest area. Instead of going on top of the car, I most likely would have gone under the car—greatly increasing the likelihood of a head or life-threatening injury.

After securing my bone fragment, the paramedics placed me on a stretcher and lifted me into the ambulance. My mother rode in the front seat of the ambulance to the hospital with me. With flashing lights and screaming sirens, we sped toward the hospital. During the loud, bumpy ride, an EMT started an IV on me and monitored my vital signs. At one point he looked at me and said, "It's just like you see on TV isn't it?" Barely conscious, I nodded and managed a half-hearted smile. Meanwhile, my dad took the mangled bicycle home, explained the situation to the rest of the family and met us at the hospital later.

After navigating through several miles of heavy traffic, we finally made our approach to St. Joseph's Hospital. We turned left off of Dale Mabry Highway onto Buffalo Avenue (the name has since changed) beside Tampa Stadium. With only a few blocks to go, we drove through the next intersection. Suddenly, a man ran a red light and smashed into the left, front fender of the ambulance. It sounded like a cannon shot. Metal mashed against metal. Glass shattered. The entire vehicle jolted from the impact. The EMT attending to me went sprawling across the cabin. Restraints on the stretcher kept me in place, but our driver was thrown into the windshield and suffered a concussion. My mother had wisely fastened her seat belt and was unharmed.

The call was made to dispatch another ambulance to complete my escort to the Emergency Room (ER). A few minutes later, I was transferred to the other ambulance in the middle of the traffic-jammed intersection.

My first driver was placed on a stretcher and rolled into the second ambulance beside me. Ironically, we rode to the ER together. Within thirty minutes I had been in two accidents. I know what you're thinking—Murphy's Law, right? What can go wrong, will go wrong! Just say it wasn't my lucky day. Seriously, I believe the devil tried to destroy me. I could have easily been killed in the first wreck if I had gone underneath the car instead of on top of it. I have pondered that possibility many times since that fateful event.

Within thirty minutes I had been in two accidents.

Though not omniscient, Satan apparently does have a limited knowledge of the future. He is aware of those who are called and anointed by God for ministry and he targets them for destruction. When the devil knows someone has potential to be used of God, he will plot their ruin any way he can. At the very least, he will try to undermine their influence.

Potential Leaders in the Crosshairs

Remember how Herod in a tyrannical rage tried to kill Jesus as an infant? (Mt. 2:16–18) Then, before Jesus began His public ministry, Satan tempted Him in the desert. It was an all-out effort to prevent Jesus from doing what God had purposed. Furthermore, think about Moses. Pharaoh made infanticide the law of the land in Egypt in an attempt to kill all the Hebrew males. But Pharaoh's daughter had pity on baby Moses when she discovered the helpless infant floating in the basket his mother, Jochebed, had made for him. Pharaoh's daughter ended up raising Moses in the palace. The one baby Pharaoh would have certainly wanted to kill was spared. As a result, God raised up Moses to humble the Egyptian Empire and deliver His people from slavery. I saw a great church sign that read, "Never give up hope—even Moses was a basket case once!" Pun intended I'm sure.

Then there was the Apostle Peter. Jesus warned him, *"Simon, Simon, behold, Satan hath desired to have you, that he may sift you as wheat...."* (Lu. 22:31 KJV) Why was the devil so intent on destroying Peter? Because he realized God was grooming him to be a powerful leader in the New Testament Church. Peter had influence. He was the kind of guy who, when he went fishing, the other disciples followed him (Jn. 21:3). Peter became the main spokesman for the disciples on the Day of Pentecost and in the early chapters of the book of Acts. And yet, approximately fifty-three days before his great Pentecost sermon that led 3,000 souls to Christ, he denied that he even knew Jesus on three occasions. Certainly Satan tried to condemn Peter and drive him to the brink of suicide just like he did Judas. What made the difference? Jesus said, *"I have prayed for you that your faith should not fail...."* (Lu. 22:32) Jesus knew Peter would fail but that his faith would carry him through. Careful study of the life of Peter reveals several major failures. But after the Day of Pentecost, this man of miracles, signs and blunders became a mighty apostle whose steady leadership pioneered the New Testament Church. Now you see why the devil fought him so much. The greater the anointing and potential you have, the bigger threat you are to Satan's kingdom and the more he wants to destroy you.

These are just three examples of leaders the devil knew would be used mightily of God. He tried in vain to dispose of them before they started their respective ministries. Similarly, the devil must have known that one day I would become a preacher and travel the country proclaiming the Gospel and winning souls. My calling was a threat to him. So he tried, unsuccessfully, to kill me. The same is true for any believers who dare to pursue God's calling for their lives. The enemy will devise schemes to discourage, discredit or destroy them before they can get started. The enemy is constantly setting snares for God's people. Jesus said, *"The thief does not come except to steal, and to kill, and to destroy…."* (Jn. 10:10) The good news is that while we are on the devil's hit list, we are also in God's witness protection program. He can foil any trap the enemy sets for us. No wonder the Psalmist wrote, *"Our soul has escaped as a bird from the snare of the fowlers; The snare is broken, and we have escaped. Our help is in the name of the Lord…."* (Ps. 124:7–8)

I see an interesting parallel between the physical and the spiritual realms. Just as my ambulance entered that dangerous intersection, I was entering an equally perilous spiritual intersection. Even at a tender age, I was making decisions that were putting me on a collision course with disaster. My life was already at a crossroads. I had to choose to either serve God, pursue His calling on my life and reap the reward, or walk the broad way of destruction and reap the inevitable consequences. The events of that day helped me make that decision. While I was unaware of it at the time, a war was being waged for my very soul.

Preventive Providence

In my opinion, only one thing kept me from being killed that day—the invisible hand of providence. Providence is the watchful care of God over and around his children. The story of Job illustrates how providence works. Satan wanted to destroy Job, but he couldn't because God had placed *"...An **hedge** about him, and about his house, and about all that he hath on every side...."* (Jb. 1:10 KJV)

That same protective hedge is around the life of every Christian and the enemy cannot penetrate it without the permission of God. I call it **preventive providence**—the protective hand of God preventing bad things from happening to you and your family. It's like a buffer zone (a force field) between you and your adversary.

I'll never forget hearing the compelling testimony of a young woman who experienced preventive providence. She was driving home after work one evening, minding her own business. A traffic light stopped her, so she waited anxiously for the light to change. Suddenly, a strange man ran up to her car, jumped in the passenger seat (she had neglected to lock her doors), pointed a gun at her and ordered, "Drive where I tell you to go!" Immediately, fear gripped her mind. She began to envision the horrible possibilities this madman could have in mind. Her knuckles turned white as she

> *Only one thing kept me from being killed that day—the invisible Hand of Providence.*

gripped the steering wheel tighter. Then the Holy Spirit quickened to her mind a portion of Scripture her pastor had preached on the previous Sunday. His text was taken from Psalm 91:4 (KJV), *"He shall cover thee with His feathers, and under His wings shalt thou trust…."* She was so shaken she couldn't recall the entire verse but one word echoed in her mind—*"Feathers!"* While she waited for the signal to turn green, with a gun still aimed at her, this woman began to say, *"Feathers, in the name of Jesus. Feathers, in the name of Jesus."* As she repeated the words, she felt a surge of boldness. So she repeated them louder. The gunman started getting nervous. Finally, the fear of God fell on him and he panicked. Jumping out of the car, he yelled, "Lady, you're crazy" and fled. The relieved woman drove home unharmed. Now that's what I mean by providence.

If we could momentarily peer into the spiritual realm, perhaps we would realize just how many disasters are averted due to an invisible hand or an angelic presence. Psalm 91:11–12 provides us with this reassurance, *"For He shall give His angels charge over you, To keep you in all your ways. In their hands they shall bear you up, lest you dash your foot against a stone."*

A song entitled *The Hand of Providence* conveys this comforting truth. I have included some of the lyrics below:

> *Providence, providence,*
> *See it laying down the cornerstone.*
> *The hand of providence, oh it's evidence*
> *That we can never make it on our own…*

Providence, ever since
Any peace has ever entered man
The hand of providence has been our best defense
Though His ways are sometimes hard to understand...

Oh the hand of providence
Is guiding us through choices that we make
Oh the hand of providence
Is reaching out to help us on our way.[1]

Permissive Providence

Every coin has two sides, so, in fairness, let's flip this coin. We all know there did come a time when God temporarily lifted the hedge that surrounded Job and allowed Satan to afflict him. Unbelievable calamity invaded his life. But God still drew a line and only permitted the devil to go so far. This is another kind of providence—**permissive providence**. This occurs when God allows tragedy in order to serve a higher purpose, often unseen at the time. It is comforting to know, as believers, that we are in God's hands. And whether it's preventive or permissive providence, God is still in control and we are not just helpless victims of circumstance. We will discuss this further in later chapters.

I believe I'm alive today only because God's hand came between me and that car on July 16, 1977. His hand was on me in the ambulance accident as well and has remained on me my entire life. Jesus said, *"My sheep...follow me...and no man is able to pluck them out of My Father's hand."* (Jn. 10:27, 29 KJV)

The Allstate Insurance Company constantly reminds its policyholders in their advertising campaigns that they are "In good hands with Allstate!" Do I have good news for you! You are in much better hands than Allstate. You are securely positioned in the

God is still in control and we are not just helpless victims of circumstance.

nail-scarred hands of Jesus! God says to all His children, *"Behold, I have graven thee upon the palms of My hands...."* (Is. 49:16 KJV) Take comfort, friend, you're in good hands. The providential hand of God forms a protective hedge between you and Satan's plots against you. To get to you, the enemy must first go through God. And *"If God be for us, who can be against us?"* (Ro. 8:31 KJV)

Negative News

Believe it or not, I did eventually make it to the hospital. The paramedics rolled me from the ambulance to the Emergency Room and transferred me to a treatment table. There the ER staff continued medical procedures on my bruised body and battered leg. I recall being shown my missing piece of bone that was placed on the counter in a jar of solution. A nurse cut off the rest of my clothes. When my pants were completely removed, one thing was observed by all present—a pack of Benson Hedges Menthol 100's (cigarettes) protruding through my underwear. *"...be sure your sin will find you out."* (Num. 32:23 KJV)

My mom was informed about the contraband. We had an interesting talk about it a few days later. Needless to say, I have never smoked again since. Someone once asked me how I quit smoking. Jokingly, I told them it was easy—I was hit by a car and it knocked the nicotine right out of me, permanently!

Careful examination of my leg revealed the extent of my injury. We were told that immediate surgery was necessary. Then a major problem presented itself. Due to the numerous boating and swimming accidents that occurred on that typically hazardous Florida Saturday, every Operating Room (OR) was occupied.

It was nearly 8:00 p.m. and time was not on our side. We were informed that with a wound of this nature "Approximately six inches in length"[2], surgery is required within so many hours or the body can be thrust into shock, creating a risky situation. Furthermore, a large quantity of debris needed to be extracted from the wound to prevent infection. Otherwise, I would be in danger of losing my leg.

While awaiting the first vacant OR, I was placed in a semi-private room to rest. My mother and a dear family friend sat at my bedside agreeing in prayer. According to the hospital schedule, the soonest opening for surgery would have been the following morning. But that would have been too late! My leg was in jeopardy. By this time many people from several churches had been informed about my accident and were interceding. Unexpectedly, and no doubt as a result of those prayers, an operating room became available. God had made a way within only four hours and at midnight I was wheeled in for surgery. How true are the words of Jesus, *"… See, I have set before you an open door, and no one can shut it…."* (Rev. 3:8)

Operation #1

During the initial operation, the three-inch section of bone dislodged from my leg was deemed unusable. That piece of bone was irreparably damaged from the impact of the collision. It was too splintered and jagged to reinsert into my shin. Instead, two metal pins were put in my leg (one just below my knee, the other just above my ankle). These pins penetrated my leg horizontally so that an inch of each was visible on either side of my leg.

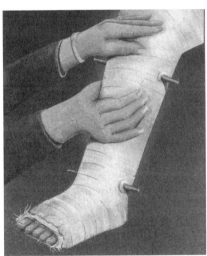

A sketch of how my leg looked in the cast and my pastor praying for me.

The wound was irrigated but left open for follow-up surgery. The uneven bone ends were trimmed and dead muscle, dirt and fat were removed. In fact, to this day my left calf muscle is visibly smaller than my right one but no less strong. They wrapped my entire leg in a plaster cast from my thigh to my toes, which also covered the four tips of the pins. A rectangular "window" was cut in the cast over the inside of my foreleg for access to dress the wound.

The following document is a recreated copy of the report from my first operation. See page 164 for an exact copy of the original.

T 7-20-77	**OPERATIVE RECORD** St. Joseph's Hospital	Godwin, Benjamin 253877 Rm828

DATE: 7-17-77

PREOPERATIVE DIAGNOSIS: Fracture, acute, traumatic, displaced, compound tibia and fibula left.

POSTOPERATIVE DIAGNOSIS: Same

OPERATION PERFORMED: [*sic*] Debriement of compound wound of left lower leg with insertion of Steinmann pins and application of long leg cast.

FINDINGS and DESCRIPTION OF OPERATION:

Under satisfactory general anesthesia, the left-leg was [*sic*] sterilly prepared and draped. The inspection of the leg revealed **an absence of [*sic*] approixmately 3 in. of midshaft of tibia and a gaping wound measuring approximately 6 in. in length** over the midshaft of the tibia over the medial side of the leg. There were lesser puncture wounds present laterally and medially. The main wound was irrigated and devitalized muscle, dirt and subcutaneous fat were excised. The wound was thoroughly irrigated with approximately 2000 cc of saline. The bone ends were trimmed of dirty material but very little bone was removed. **There had been previous loss of considerable amount of bone, approximately 3 inches.** The wound was allowed to fall together. No sutures were used except for the ligatures of bleeding points. [*sic*] Adaptic was placed over the exposed muscle. The fascia of the gastroc was incised. The two Steinmann pins were driven across the tibia, both proximally and distally to the fracture site and traction was applied to the leg and a long leg cast applied. The patient was sent to the recovery room in satisfactory condition. Complications: None.

The plan is to return the patient to the OR and do a secondary closure of this wound in a few days if infection does not [*sic*] insue.

D 7-17-77   M J. MILLER, M. D./ch

After surgery, I was moved to the recovery room where I drifted in and out of consciousness in an anesthetic stupor. At this time, my orthopedic surgeon, Richard J. Miller, M.D., relayed to my parents the "negative news." He gave them a brief summary of the operation. He explained that I had an acute, traumatic, compound fracture to both my tibia and fibula and that three inches of my tibia was displaced. Furthermore, I would require bone graft surgery, in which bone would be taken from my hip and implanted into my shin. He raised the possibility of amputation, the probability of wearing a cast for up to two years, being confined to a wheelchair for months and my left leg always being an inch or so shorter than my right leg. In short, he tried to brace my parents for the reality that, at best, I would never walk again without a severe limp or, at worst, I might even need a prosthetic limb.

The words of this well-meaning doctor fell on deaf ears. My mom and dad are people of very strong faith. They have witnessed and experienced many miracles and they simply disregarded this report in their hearts. They began to speak and claim the Word of God. They believed God for a miracle and a complete recovery of the use of my leg. But there was still a long, uphill climb with many battles ahead.

Operation #2

Five days later, July 22, 1977, I was still hospitalized and sent in for a second operation. This was a relatively brief procedure. They had to operate through the window that had been previously cut in my cast. They performed a primary closure of the wound. My surgeon looked carefully for any signs of infection. "The skin edges were approximated...the wound was dressed and appeared to be remarkably clean."[3]

The following document is a recreated copy of the report from my second operation. See page 165 for an exact copy of the original.

T 7-26-77	**OPERATIVE RECORD** St. Joseph's Hospital	Godwin, Benjamin 253877-4

DATE: July 22, 1977   **SURGEON:** Richard Miller, M.D.

PREOPERATIVE DIAGNOSIS: Healing soft tissue wound with compound fracture of the left tibia and fibula.

POSTOPERATIVE DIAGNOSIS: Same

OPERATION PERFORMED: Delayed primary closure of wound.

FINDINGS and DESCRIPTION OF OPERATION:

Under satisfactory general anesthesia, operating through the window in the previously applied cast, the wound was dressed and appeared to be remarkably clean. The skin edges were approximated except for a one square inch of loss of skin under which overlying the medial head of the gastrocnemius muscle. This was not grafted.

An adaptor dressing was applied and sterile dressing was applied and the patient was sent to the recovery room in good condition.

D 7-22-77 Richard Miller, M. D./ab

Operation #3

Seven days later, July 29, 1977, I was still hospitalized and faced yet a third surgery. By this time the wound had granulated (small fleshy beads had formed on the surface of the wound) indicating the healing process had begun. During this operation, a split thickness skin graft was removed from my right thigh with a battery-operated dermatome. The skin graft measured two square inches and was sutured over the granulating wound with nylon stitches. Some stainless steel sutures inserted in one of the previous operations were also removed.

The following document is a recreated copy of the report from my third operation. See page 166 for an exact copy of the original.

T 8-1-77 V	**OPERATIVE RECORD** St. Joseph's Hospital	Godwin, Benjamin 253877 Rm828

DATE: 7-29-77   SURGEON: Richard Miller, M.D.

PREOPERATIVE DIAGNOSIS: Granulating wound left leg.

POSTOPERATIVE DIAGNOSIS: Same

OPERATION PERFORMED: Split thickness graft right thigh to left shin.

FINDINGS and DESCRIPTION OF OPERATION:

Under satisfactory general anesthesia the left-leg and right hip were [*sic*] sterilly prepared. Operating through a window in the left cast the granulating wound was found to measure approximately 2 in. square. A split thickness graft using the battery operated dermatome was removed from the right thigh. This was sutured in place over the granulating wound. Some of the stainless steel sutures previously inserted were removed. Some additional nylon sutures were placed across the previous wound and the split thickness graft was punctured with numerous slits and sutured in place with nylon. [*sic*] Adaptic dressing was placed on both wounds and the patient was sent to the recovery room in good condition. Blood loss [*sic*] negligable. Prognosis for wound healing is good. The patient will require further surgery on the bone of the left leg.

D 7-29-77/ R. S. MILLER, M. D./cb

While I was in the hospital, many friends from our church and neighborhood brought balloons, get-well cards and other gifts. Two ministers were specifically led of the Lord to my bedside with words of encouragement for my parents and me. One of these pastors received a word of knowledge that my leg was going to be restored by a miracle. The other minister told us of a vision the Lord had given him in which he saw my leg completely healed. My parents clung to these confirmations of God's Word tenaciously. Whenever they heard a negative report they just kept praying, believing and standing on the promises of God.

A couple of times a day a family member or a nurse strolled me around the pediatric wing of the hospital in a wheelchair. I met and talked to several other kids who were there for treatment for various problems. One special friend I met, Andy, stands out in my mind. Both of his legs and an arm had been broken when he was struck by a dump truck. He had a cast on both of his legs connected by a bar between his knees. We bonded so well because of the similarity of our accidents. Besides, we had a lot in common. We were both scheduled to undergo bone graft surgery. My parents witnessed to his parents a lot and we all prayed for Andy many times. It was really interesting to see how God used my parents to minister to several other couples whose kids were in similar predicaments.

After eighteen days of being a hospital "hostage," I was eager to go home.

After eighteen days of being a hospital "hostage," I was eager to go home. While the nurses were nice and I was allowed to watch more television than normal, still I grew weary of hospital food, shots, bedpans, IV's and being bed-ridden. I was ready to return to my house and to my life for that matter. I wanted to be a kid again.

Everything was moving too slowly as far as I was concerned. I had come down with a bad case of cabin fever and/or homesickness.

On August 2, 1977, I was given an "honorable discharge" from St. Joseph's Hospital.

The following document is a recreated copy of the my discharge summary. See page 167 for an exact copy of the original.

T 8-19-77 IX **DISCHARGE SUMMARY** Godwin, Benjamin D.

253877

Format: Date of admission and of discharge; 2) provisional diagnosis; 3) brief history; 4) pertinent physical and laboratory findings; 5) course and treatment; 6) condition on discharge-ambulant, etc.7) follow-up care and discharge medication-name and dosage; 8) final diagnosis.

ADMITTED: 7-16-77   DISCHARGED: 8-2-77

The patient was admitted to the hospital through the E.R. following an accident in which he was struck by a car on a bicycle. This resulted in a compound fracture of the left tibia and fibula with a loss of approximately 3 inches of the shaft of the tibia.

He underwent immediate debridement. The wound was left open. He was placed in a long leg cast with pins above and below. Subsequent to this he was returned to the operating room a few days later and secondary closure of the wound was obtained. Some of the skin was lost and could not be approximated so that he then had a split thickness graft to cover an area approximately 2 square inches over the medial side of the calf.

At the time of discharge there was approximately 1 sq. cm. of bone exposed in the distal fragment. This will require further treatment.

He was discharged in a long leg cast with the pins above and below. He will be followed as an outpatient, and will have to return for further surgery. It is planned to do a bone graft following wound closure.

signature

D 8-17-77   RICHARD MILLER, M.D./mb

Did you notice the last paragraph of the discharge summary? It reads, *"He was discharged in a long leg cast with pins above and below. He will be followed as an outpatient, and will have to return for further surgery. It is planned to perform **a bone graft** following wound closure."*[4] We were told by Dr. Miller that bone would be removed from my hip/thigh vicinity and implanted into my shin. Pins, plates and screws would hold the bones in place while they slowly grew back together. Still, with these corrective measures, the surgeon could only speculate on the long-term usefulness of my leg. Furthermore, after the bone graft, we were told to expect months of rehab therapy.

Home Sweet Home

Finally, I returned home for the first time in nearly a month, only under very different circumstances than when I left. My leg was in a cast and my body was in a wheelchair. My life had totally changed. All the little things I took for granted now became a challenge.

Taking a bath, for instance, was a real adventure. I couldn't take a shower because my cast could not get wet. So to take a bath I had to situate myself in the tub with my left leg propped up on the side. Getting dressed was also a major task. None of my pants fit over the bulky cast, especially with the two pins sticking out an inch on both sides. My mom customized some of my clothes. She cut the left leg of all my pants off at the knee. Then she cut the inseam up to the crotch. Along the open seam she sewed in Velcro so the pant leg would close together over the top part of my bulky cast.

My parents rented a miniature wheelchair for me. I had lots of fun doing wheelies down the hallway. While I was in my wheelchair, in bed or just sitting in a regular chair, I always had to have my left leg extended straight out in front of me and elevated. Otherwise, it would throb and the pain would be unbearable. My cast wouldn't permit my knee to bend.

I celebrated my eighth birthday on August 18, 1977. I don't remember much about my party but I do recall a gift my dad bought me—a digital watch. These were a popular, new fad in the late 70's. I was fascinated by it because it displayed the date as well as the time. It also had a stop watch feature on it. I used it to time how many seconds I could hold my breath. And, best of all, it had a light so you could tell the time in the dark. That was such a "cool" gift, I thought.

Good Old Golden Rule Days

Late August came around and the school year began. My parents switched my brother, Jesse, and me to a small, private school called Gospel Assembly. The school was run on the Accelerated Christian Education curriculum, which allows students of all ages and grades to be in the same, large classroom. Each student had workbooks in various subjects on his or her grade level.

The desks were small cubicles with dividers on either side fastened along the perimeter walls of the pre-fab building. Several self-supporting rows of desks were lined across the middle of the room. The problem I had was that the desks didn't allow enough clearance space for my leg underneath. So they placed a card table at the very front of the classroom under which I could fit my leg.

It served as my very own custom desk. From that vantage point, I was able to survey the entire classroom.

Incidentally, I started attending Gospel Assembly that year (1977) in third grade. Ten years later, I graduated from the same school. I owe a great debt of gratitude to my former and late principal, M. B. Babbitt, and former head-teacher, Carolyn Babbitt, and all of the other teachers who invested their time in my life. The opportunities and training they gave me not only helped prepare me for life but for the ministry as well. What I am today is largely due to their influence and willingness to invest their lives in mine. Too many fond memories to recount were produced on that campus. I still cherish my Class of '87 high school ring.

Each morning when I arrived at school, a senior named Tim Quinn, who later worked in my dad's business for many years, pulled my wheelchair out of the back of our station wagon. Then he helped me get into it and rolled me into the classroom. I remember how fun it was to get so much attention from my classmates. During breaks and lunch hour, they argued over who got to push my wheelchair. Many friends signed my cast or drew pictures on it.

After wearing my cast for several weeks, it became a nuisance. It was heavy and ugly for starters. Then it became itchy. I frequently used a butter knife to scratch the dead skin off of the bottom of my foot. To make matters worse, our Florida weather made it hot and sweaty. Then it began to stink very badly. It was very embarrassing too. Before I left home each day, I sprayed it down with some brand of aerosol deodorant.

Still, during class, I would notice kids wrinkle their noses and whisper when they were around me.

When physical education time came around each day, reality set in like salt in an open wound. While my friends played football or kickball, I rolled up and down the parking lot next to the field watching, longing to jump up and join them. It was hard to accept that it was no longer physically possible.

Many times I wondered if I would ever be normal again. Even after the bone graft operation, would I be able to play with my friends like I used to? Would I be able to run, jump or even walk without a limp? Or would I always be confined to a wheelchair or a pair of crutches? At eight years of age, I was already experiencing the frustrations of a handicapped body that simply could not do what my mind wanted it to do. Would I really be a semi-cripple the rest of my life as my pessimistic doctor predicted? I desperately hoped that would not be the case. If so, how could life be so cruel? And why me anyway? I hate to admit it but I was feeling sorry for myself. I should have been thankful just to be alive. Now, whenever I feel like life isn't fair, I remind myself of a saying my father-in-law, Rev. Raymond Bolton, used to share in his sermons,

I once met a man who felt sorry for himself
because he had no shoes,
until he met a man who had no feet!

Take a look around. You can always find someone with far worse problems than your own. We would all do well to replace the habit of complaining with the habit of being thankful. Most of all, remember this—even when the news is bad, God is still good!

The Missing Ingredient

An uneventful month drifted by with no discernible changes. By the first part of September, 1977, I was still confined to a wheelchair and three inches of bone was still missing from my leg. Due to recurring pain and frequent doctor appointments, I was absent from school nearly as many days as I was present during the first semester.

The bone graft operation loomed over me like an ominous cloud. Meanwhile, my doctor office visits became very predictable. After thirty minutes or so of boredom in the waiting room, my name would be called and an assistant escorted my mother and me to an examination room. Another brief wait usually ensued. Finally, my orthopedist, Dr. Miller, would arrive, greet us and unwind the ACE wrap covering the window on my cast. Then he'd remove the sullied gauze and dressings. He always examined the wound carefully, looking for signs of infection. Also, he observed how my skin graft was growing into the original skin around the wound. Dr. Miller would then order a new set of x-rays to be taken. A nurse normally dressed my wound with sterile dressing and re-wrapped my entire foreleg with a new ACE bandage. When the new set of x-rays were developed, the doctor would return to explain them to my mother and I. Each one was like a broken record, blaring out the same disappointing tune—three inches of bone were still missing without any indication of progress.

Right in the middle of this whole crisis, my parents were led of the Lord to remove me from Dr. Miller's care. He was definitely a gifted specialist and, no doubt, is to be credited with saving my leg during the initial operations. However, he was also a profane unbeliever and spoke very derogatorily to my parents whenever they brought up the possibility of divine intervention of any kind. They didn't want me under his influence a day longer after he insulted their faith one time too many. So the search began for a new orthopedic surgeon.

A New Orthopedist

My parents prayed to be led by the Holy Spirit to the right orthopedist. In the meantime, they set up an appointment with an interim doctor to ensure my wound received proper care. Dr. Reed was, and is to this day, a family friend and a Spirit-filled Christian. Up to this time, I had never seen my wound. Usually, when it was dressed at the doctor's office or by my parents, I was laying down on either a treatment table or a bed. In Dr. Reed's office, however, I was sitting upright in my wheelchair when he removed the bandages. Not only was it a gruesome looking wound, but as my hospital records indicate, "There was approximately one square centimeter of bone exposed"[5] near my ankle that the skin graft had not covered. Just one look was all it took! I turned my head immediately. I felt light-headed, nauseous and dizzy. I nearly fainted. Later, I grew accustomed to seeing my unsightly leg.

Dr. Reed was able to give my parents some advice and also recommended another orthopedic surgeon, Dr. Vega. My first appointment with Dr. Vega was on September 15, 1977. He prescribed a pair of crutches for me to maneuver around on, provided I promised not to put any weight on my injured leg. After two months in a wheelchair it was a welcome change. Dr. Vega treated me the rest of the way through this ordeal until the spring of 1978.

A Life-changing Tent Revival

By this time, churches all over Florida were praying for "little Ben." A network of intercession was "transmitted" daily, filling the throne room of grace with petitions. My parents requested prayer from every known source. We attended numerous healing services in the vicinity of Tampa, believing God for a miracle. One particular tent meeting comes to mind. Evangelist Mike Shreve was conducting this revival. At the conclusion of his sermon, I hobbled on my crutches up to the altar to receive prayer for my leg. I began to pray with all the sincerity I could muster. While Bro. Shreve prayed for me that night, I was baptized with the Holy Spirit. Warm tears streamed down my cheeks as I prayed in a heavenly language. I returned home that night with the same broken leg but also with something else— a renewed heart.

That night was a turning point in my life. From then on I had a desire to travel with *that* preacher and do what he was doing. My wish came true when I was thirteen. My parents let me travel with Bro. Shreve during the summer months. I continued to do so for the following five summers. Then, two days after graduating from high school in 1987, I went on the road full-time with Mike Shreve and began working in the ministry as his understudy. I owe an enormous debt of gratitude to him because of the opportunities he has afforded me in ministry. He is my mentor and Father in the Lord, much like Paul was to Timothy.

Around this same time, our family attended our home church one Sunday as usual, but this particular Sunday was different. During the service, one of our church elders was inspired to pray for me. He laid his hands on me and began to intercede. As he sought God on my behalf, my mother, who was standing nearby, received a vision from the Lord. She beheld an x-ray of my leg. It was identical to the ones the doctors had shown us. It was obvious that three inches of bone were missing. Suddenly, a thread-like, milky-white substance appeared, spanning the gap from the upper bone end to the lower bone end. Gradually, the bony substance expanded until it completely filled in the vacant area. This vision later proved to be prophetic in nature, revealing how God would eventually restore my leg.

The Faith Pool Prayer Group

October rolled around and I was still in the same condition. On Friday, October 7, 1977, I went to school as usual and our family attended a prayer meeting that evening at our pastor's house. (My parents attended these Friday night prayer meetings faithfully for nearly thirty years.)

Our pastor, Bertha Madden, was a seventy-nine year old widow at the time. She had been a prominent Sunday School teacher and traveling youth speaker in a large church in Tampa. When she received the baptism of the Holy Spirit with the evidence of speaking in tongues, she was dismissed from all of her leadership positions. Misunderstood and ostracized, she didn't know what to do or where to go. Then God spoke to her to start a prayer meeting in her home. So with four people present in January of 1957, the *Faith Pool Prayer Group* was founded. Many of her former students, my mother included, came to her for teaching on the Holy Spirit. They began regularly attending Bertha Madden's "forbidden" prayer meetings. Many of them were healed and baptized with the Spirit. As the prayer meeting grew, a church was established. For several years this church met in Bertha Madden's home until God blessed them to build a sanctuary. They moved in under the name *House of Hope*. That was the church our family attended as my siblings and I grew up.

When we arrived that Friday night, the prayer meeting was already in progress. The prayer room was a simple, cinder-block addition built on to Mrs. Madden's house. As we entered, I glanced at the familiar people who were gathered for prayer. I followed my parents across the room and slumped down on one of the many outdated couches that lined the room. I set my crutches on the floor. To say that my nearly three-month-old, dirt-stained, ink-marked, pin-protruding cast was conspicuous would be an understatement. It had been autographed by so many of my friends that it looked more like a graffiti-marred wall in the ghetto than a medical apparatus. Frankly, it was an eyesore! My five pale toes hung out the end which I wiggled now and then to entertain myself.

A Night to Remember

Everyone present that memorable night was praying except me. I restlessly squirmed in my seat for about thirty minutes. Then the atmosphere changed. A sweeping spirit of travail and intercession filled the room. The presence of God seemed to hover over us like a canopy. It was as if Jesus Himself was walking among us.

Incidentally, when the Lord spoke to Mrs. Madden to start the prayer group back in 1957, the Lord showed her a vision in which she saw her living room filled with people kneeling in intercession. As they prayed, Jesus walked among them touching them and blessing them. It was that kind of night! Many present, including my pastor, began to weep without reservation. Composure and dignity were the least of her concerns as she dropped to the floor on her hands and knees. She crawled to my side of the room

"A new bone for Ben! Oh God, honor your Word with a new bone in this leg."

on very thin, commercial-grade carpet. There was no padding between the carpet and the concrete slab underneath. For some reason, I had this uncanny notion that she was coming directly to me.

She kept praying in the Spirit as she knelt at my feet. Gripped with compassion, it was as if her leg, not mine, was inactive and immobile. She wept as though she was the one experiencing the pain. As she bent close to my leg, tears glistened on her aged, faith-filled face. She stroked my plaster cast with trembling hands. It was a simple but powerfully effective prayer. My pastor desperately cried, "A new bone for Ben! Oh, God, honor Your Word with a new bone in this leg." When she prayed, I felt something move inside my leg. I had no idea what really happened, but it felt as if an invisible hand reached down and placed a NEW BONE into my shin. *"...The effective, fervent prayer of a righteous man avails much."* (Ja. 5:16)

The Breakthrough

Would this prayer, along with the hundreds of other prayers, finally bring the breakthrough? Sometimes prayer can be like hammering through concrete. It takes numerous blows to get through to the other side. One person can swing a sledge hammer several times without penetrating the concrete. Then another person, in relief of the exhausted person, can swing just a few times and suddenly the concrete gives way. It wasn't the last swing that did all the work. It was all the other blows that loosened the concrete so the last one could breakthrough. Literally hundreds of people prayed for me, including Sister Madden on several previous occasions. Pastor Madden just happened to be the one God used to finish the job at that particular time. Why? I don't know. But I'm sure glad it worked out that way.

Pastor Madden's prayer, combined with all the others, overruled all the well-meaning opinions of doctors. It nullified the suffering that they said I would inevitably face. Instead, God masterfully performed a divine bone graft without an incision. My trek from a wheelchair to the pulpit was now underway.

When the prayer meeting ended that night, I maneuvered to our car on my crutches. As we traveled home, I told my parents, "When Pastor Madden prayed for me, I felt something *move* in my leg." We all believed God had done something miraculous, we just didn't have the proof, at least not yet! None of us were fully aware of what had happened that night. It was yet to be discovered and is yet to be told in the following chapter. Before I share the good report, I want to re-emphasize an extremely important ingredient in the working of healing and miracles—compassion.

Compassion: The Key Ingredient

Compassion is defined as *"The deep feeling of sharing the suffering of another, together with the inclination to give aid or support or show mercy."*[6] Our English word *compassion* is derived from two Latin words: *Com* meaning "with" and *patti* meaning "to suffer."[7] Combining the two, compassion is simply rendered "to suffer with another."

Sometimes, in the Body of Christ, there tends to be an over emphasis on faith and confession when it comes to receiving healing. Don't get me wrong, faith is vital, *"Without faith it is impossible to please God."* (Heb. 11:6 KJV) And we certainly can and should claim and confess the promises of God. But there are some instances in Scripture where people either had little or no faith and God still performed a miracle in their behalf. Some people Jesus healed came to Him believing for a miracle and were rewarded: Jairus—Mk. 5:22, the Centurion—Mt. 8:5–7, the Woman with the Issue of Blood—Mt. 9:22, etc. Others Jesus healed weren't even seeking for Jesus to heal them but He healed them anyway: the Impotent Man at the Pool of Bethesda—Jn. 5:1–8, the Man Born Blind—Jn. 9:1–7, Legion, the demon-possessed man from Gadara—Mt. 8:28–34, etc.

My point is that God is Sovereign. He can do what He wants, when He wants, where He wants, with whom He wants—all without our permission. He often does things that run against the grain of our narrow-minded theology. God is too big to fit in our neat little theological boxes. Consequently, there is no fixed formula that always works for healing. There are too many exceptions. It is a gross oversimplification to automatically attribute cases in which people do not get healed to a lack of faith. There are too many other factors involved.

Often, in Jesus' ministry, His compassion was the determining factor for the needy in receiving healing, not their own abundance or lack of faith. In fact, there are at least fourteen instances in the Gospels in which Jesus was touched or moved with compassion toward various people. Thereafter, in a pattern-like way, He would heal their sickness, feed them

> *I believe compassion is a missing ingredient in the modern church's quest for miracles.*

or minister to their spiritual needs. Compassion compelled Him to action. Faith was often an important factor, but it wasn't the only factor.

God's Motive for Healing

Consider the lacerations on Jesus' body that procured our healing. Many believe Jesus was whipped thirty-nine times (forty stripes was the maximum allowed under Moses' Law—Dt. 25:3). Out of "mercy" it was common for the Jews to whip a criminal with thirty-nine lashes. (See 2 Cor. 11:24.) However, we must remember that it was not the Jews who flogged Jesus; it was the Romans and they were not bound by Jewish Law. Imagine a whip consisting of a short handle from which leather thongs extended, each lined with chips of bone, stone, metal or other sharp objects. This sadistic instrument of torture was designed solely to inflict pain. When the whip made contact, it literally shredded the flesh right off the bones. Thus, literally hundreds of lacerations brutalized Jesus' broken body—all for our healing. *"...With his stripes we are healed."* (Is. 53:5 KJV) To avoid undue gore, paintings of the crucifixion merely show a few trickles of blood streaming from Jesus' wounds. In reality, Jesus was beaten beyond recognition—*"...His visage* [appearance] *was so marred more than any man...."* (Is. 52:14 KJV) Why did He endure the torture of the cross? Out of His compassion for lost mankind.

When you evaluate why God heals the sick, the bottom line is this: God loves to alleviate the pain and suffering of His people. God never intended for sickness to be in this world to begin with. He certainly didn't create it that way. Sickness is a result of the original sin of Adam and Eve and will remain a stark reality of human existence until Jesus returns. In my opinion,

God doesn't heal the sick in order to validate a ministry or to vindicate a doctrinal persuasion. He heals simply because it hurts Him to see His children suffer. *"For we have not a high priest which cannot be **touched with the feeling of our infirmities**...."* (Heb. 4:15 KJV) When we hurt, God hurts! If you stub your toe, your entire body feels the throbbing pain. In the body of Christ, when a member is sick, Jesus—the head of the body—is aware of it and commiserates with the wounded member.

Faith, Hope, Love

This in no way minimizes the important role faith plays in healing. It simply affirms that *"Faith works by love."* (Gal. 5:6) You see, it is impossible to have true compassion without giving of yourself in some measure to benefit others. My pastor, Bertha Madden, got to the point where she prayed for me just like she would have prayed for herself if she were in my condition. Praying for someone to be healed in order to showcase our faith is the wrong motive. But praying for someone to be healed with the same motive Jesus had when he provided for our healing—a genuine desire to see them relieved of suffering—is true compassion. As an eight year-old boy, I had a child-like faith to be healed, even though I didn't understand all the truths about divine healing. But my pastor's faith, mingled with compassion, touched the heart of God. In return, He touched me.

I believe compassion is a missing ingredient in the modern church's quest for miracles. As the church begins to demonstrate the compassion of Jesus toward the afflicted, we will see more miracles. God is certainly not reluctant to heal. Why would Jesus go to such an extreme measure to provide for our healing and then be unwilling to administer it? God wants to heal the sick more than we want Him to. *"Fear not little flock; for it is your Father's good pleasure to give you the kingdom."* (Lu. 12:32 KJV) Healing is one of the many benefits of the Kingdom. There is no limit to what God can do when He finds a yielded vessel with a pure heart and the right motives. *"And now abide faith, hope, love, these three; but the greatest of these is love."* (1 Cor. 13:13)

> *Out of the greatest love He bled,*
> *Compassioned for man He died,*
> *To administer the children's bread,*
> *Yes, healing virtue He supplied.*

A Bone-a-fide Miracle

Our entire prayer group sensed that something wonderful had happened in my leg. All we needed was medical confirmation. My next appointment was scheduled for November 3, 1977. My mom and I arrived at the doctor's office brimming with expectation. We sat eagerly in the waiting room until a doctor's assistant called for me. She led me directly to the x-ray room while my mom waited in an examination room. I wore a heavy, lead-filled vest in the x-ray room to shield me from exposure to radiation. The assistant instructed me to turn my leg as she shot the x-rays from various angles.

After the x-ray session, I joined my mother in the examination room to await the doctor. Before long, he entered the room and greeted us with cordial gestures. When he sat down, his smiles quickly faded. He expressed grave concern about the fact that we had skipped two previous appointments. My last appointment had been September 15, 1977.

This appointment was on November 3, 1977. So for a total of forty-eight days I had not seen a doctor with my leg in such poor condition. The doctor scolded my mom for her "irresponsibility." She explained to him that the Lord had spoken to her that I would be healed soon. My mom trusted the Lord to do just that by giving Him time to work a miracle without the doctor's interference. When the doctor heard Mom's explanation, he was livid. He lit into my mom with a flurry of medical rationale, sprinkled with a few expletives for emphasis. "Mrs. Godwin," he said at one point, "Don't you understand that infection or gangrene could set in and Ben could lose his leg?" Gulp! His words, like a pin puncturing a balloon, deflated our hopeful spirits. In frustration, he whirled around and closed the door with authority. He went to examine my new x-rays. We sat silently for a few moments—stunned!

Faith Rewarded

Questioningly, I glanced at Mom. She, in turn, grasped my hand and began to pray. In a soft but determined whisper, Mom prayed something like this "...I bind you, Satan, and all of your accusations against us in the name of Jesus. Lord, you have promised to restore this leg by a miracle. We've trusted you this far and we are not giving up now...." Quietly, we sat there praying under our breath. A few minutes later, the doctor returned. We braced ourselves for more verbal abuse. But something was noticeably different about him. His countenance had changed and he wasn't angry with us anymore. He didn't lash out in harsh words. Frankly, he appeared dumbfounded. "Uh...um...Mrs. Godwin," he stuttered, "I don't know how to explain this, but something has changed in Ben's leg since you were here last." Our eyes widened with hope. The doctor then led us down the hall to the x-ray room. I hobbled along as fast as I could on my crutches.

All three of us crowded around the lighted x-ray screen. Dr. Vega pulled out his pointer and was about to explain it to us when my mom saw *it*. She asked, "Is that what I think it is?" All it took was a nod of the doctor's head and she blurted out

> *I tugged on Mama's shoulder and said, "He did it, Mom, Jesus really did it!"*

"Hallelujah!" The doctor, in medical terms, tried to explain that mysteriously three inches of bone appeared on the new x-rays. The gap of missing bone wasn't filled in solidly, but a thin shaft of bone was visible connecting the two bone ends.

When I caught on to what had happened, I tugged on Mama's shoulder and said, "He did it, Mom, Jesus really did it!" About that time, Mom started literally leaping for joy. Her hands shot up in the air and she began praising the Lord. Tears of joy streamed down our faces. The doctor was blocked into the corner of the room and was unable to do anything but watch us celebrate. Baffled by the whole thing, he looked at my mom and conceded, "Mrs. Godwin, you really do have faith." We couldn't wait to tell my dad and our pastor the good news.

We were still rejoicing as the doctor scheduled me to meet him at St. Joseph's Hospital the very next day, November 4, 1977. Since bone graft surgery was no longer necessary, Dr. Vega took off my old cast and removed the two pins from my leg. A fresh cast was placed on my leg to protect the tender areas from injury while my leg strengthened. I only had to wear it for twenty-four days. It was replaced with a half cast to my knee on November 28, 1977. By then I could walk freely without crutches. As foretold in the vision my mother received, my leg was gradually, but totally, restored.

Though hardly a Christian, my doctor was nominally religious. When he saw the undeniable miracle in my leg and such a genuine witness in my mom, he began to change. In fact, my mother had a housekeeper at the time who was also employed by my doctor. She informed us that Dr. Vega began reading the Bible and attending a Bible-believing church. The last we heard he has maintained his resolutions.

The New Bone Rebroken

Don't think for a moment the enemy took all this sitting down. Over the years since my miracle, he has sought tirelessly to annul my testimony. One such occasion occurred during the Christmas Holidays of 1977. I was out in our yard with one of my brothers and a neighbor tossing the football. I still had my half cast on but I could move about pretty well. Progressively, we got rougher. Before long we were tackling each other. While I had the ball, our neighbor friend jumped on my back to tackle me. The extra weight caused my cast-encased leg to jam into the ground. Instantly, acute pain shot through my leg. On January 5, 1978, my mom took me back to Dr. Vega. An x-ray revealed that I had fractured my "new bone." I missed two solid weeks of school and was in constant agony. But in a few weeks the bone mended perfectly and my testimony was preserved.

The complete restoration of my leg is what I call a "BONE-a-fide" miracle, pun intended. Throughout junior high and high school, I was very involved in athletics. I played basketball, football, softball, volleyball, soccer, water skied, roller skated, etc. I won various athletic awards from my school and from the Florida State Accelerated Christian Education Convention for competition in ping pong and basketball. If God had not performed a miracle in my leg, there is no possible way I could have done any of those activities.

Today, I do not have a limp. My legs are the same length. I have the full use of my leg without any pain whatsoever. I never did have a bone graft operation. My doctors told me I would be semi-crippled the rest of my life, but God intervened and gave me a NEW BONE by a creative miracle.

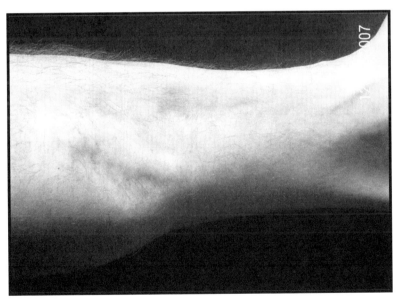

This is a picture of the leg and what it actually looks like today with the surgical scars.

X-RAY #1 (before)

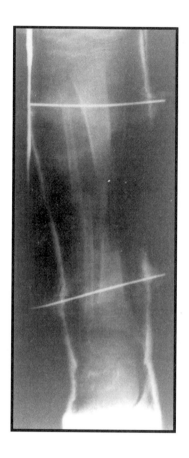

This is a view from the back of my left leg. Notice the heel of my foot at the bottom. The three-inch piece of missing bone is clearly visible on the Tibia (the large bone on the right). Some of what may appear to be bone is actually "A large area of soft tissue swelling and dressing over the anterior (front) portion of the tibia," according to my hospital records. You can also see the fracture to the Fibula (the smaller bone on the left). The two white lines running horizontally across the x-ray are the pins that were placed through my leg to hold it in place. This x-ray was taken on September 15, 1977—two months after my accident.

X-RAY #2 (after)

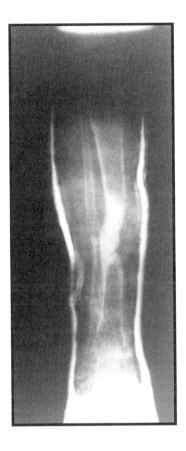

This view was taken a few months after the miracle transpired. You can see how the former gap is solidly filled in with new bone (bright white). Remember, I never had bone graft surgery of any kind. What you are looking at is the sovereign handiwork of God. This was the final x-ray ever taken of my leg. After this x-ray was taken on March 6, 1978, I have not seen a doctor for any reason regarding this leg.

X-RAY #3

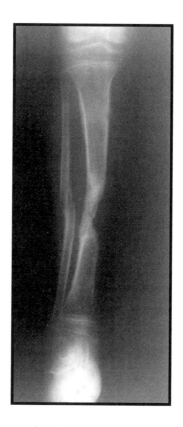

This x-ray was taken on January 5, 1978. It shows how my miracle bone was fractured during the friendly football game mentioned earlier. It mended back properly with rest and prayer, thus preserving my testimony intact.

A Higher Calling

When I received my miracle, my pastor and my parents sensed a call of God on my life to preach. None of them told me about it at the time. In retrospect, they were wise not to do so and I'm glad they didn't, because I discovered it for myself in the summer of 1983 when I was thirteen years old. That July, I asked my parents if I could travel with Evangelist Mike Shreve until school started. They consented and I traveled to Tennessee, North Carolina, West Virginia and Virginia that summer helping to set up a large Gospel tent for crusades and playing drums in the nightly services.

When I returned home in August, Pastor Madden asked me to give a report on what I had done during the summer to our church. She also asked me to preach for a few minutes. There were probably only about fifty people present that night, but I felt like I was Billy Graham in a packed-out stadium. That night, I preached my first sermon. From then

There were probably only about fifty people present that night, but I felt like I was Billy Graham in a packed-out stadium.

on until I graduated from high school in 1987, Sis. Madden asked me to preach once a month on Sunday nights. Between the coaching and experience she and my teachers at my Christian school gave me, it was great hands-on ministry training. Both my church and my school served as launching pads for my ministry.

Two days after graduating from high school, I went on the road full-time with Evangelist Mike Shreve and continued training under his ministry for the next four years. Then in September of 1990, I began evangelizing on my own. I continued in traveling ministry until August of 1994 when I accepted a position as Assistant Pastor at the Goodsprings Full Gospel Church (thirty miles West of Birmingham, Alabama). Then in February of 1999, I became the pastor upon the retirement of my father-in-law who had pastored the church for thirty-three years. During my years of ministry, I have been blessed to preach in hundreds of churches in over half of the United States. I have also made a few missionary trips out of the country to Costa Rica, Canada, Mexico and Russia. The Lord has blessed this ministry with many souls. I still travel on a limited scale as a guest speaker in churches, conferences, youth camps and schools.

My testimony is that God's healing power is real! I am compelled to share the message of hope that *"Jesus Christ* [is] *the same yesterday, and today, and forever."* (Heb. 13:8 KJV) In other words, what Jesus did 2,000 years ago during His earthly ministry, He still does today. If He saved then, He saves now. If He healed then, He heals now. If He baptized with the Holy Spirit then, He hasn't changed. God is no respecter of persons. He doesn't show partiality or favoritism. He loves all of His children the same—unconditionally. All we need to do is get in a receptive position to receive what He already wants to give us. God is not only *able* to heal, He is *willing* and *eager* to heal. He's looking for someone to take Him at His Word.

Is It God's Will to Heal?

Scripture is very clear about God's will concerning healing. God wants His children healed and healthy. Consider this verse: *"...Thy **will** be done in earth, as it is in heaven."* (Mt. 6:10 KJV) Obviously there is no sickness in heaven. In what is commonly known as the Lord's Prayer, Jesus instructs us to pray that the will of God will be performed here on earth just like it is in heaven. If there are no sick people in heaven, then it is God's will that there be no sick people on earth, especially among His own children. Of course, we know there will be sickness in this realm until Jesus returns and completely lifts the curse of sin off of this world and the sickness that results from that sin. But we must believe that it is God's will for us to be healed. *"Beloved, I pray that you may prosper in all things and be in health, just as your soul prospers."* (3 Jn. 2)

Being a parent, one of the hardest things for me to see is my own children in pain. Naturally I want to do everything in my power to bring them relief when they are sick. Just think, if we as humans are inclined to aid our suffering offspring, how much more does God desire to intervene in the behalf of His children? Jesus said, *"If you then, being evil, know how to give good gifts to your children, **how much more** will your Father who is in heaven give good things to those who ask Him!"* (Mt. 7:11)

When Jesus was approached by a leper (Mt. 8:2–3), the man said, *"Lord, if You are willing, You can make me clean."* Jesus simply replied, *"**I am willing**; be cleansed."* Immediately, his leprosy disappeared. In essence, Jesus said, "It is my will for you to be healed." If it was His will for that leper then, why wouldn't it be the same for us today? God does not change! Obviously, not everyone gets healed and God's will is not always accomplished. The Bible emphatically states that God is *"...Not **willing** that any should perish, but that all should come to repentance."* (2 Pt. 3:9 KJV) We know that only a minority of the human race will actually be saved compared to the masses adrift on the broad way to destruction. (See Mt. 7:13–14.) But it is God's will that **all** be saved. You see, there are things that can prevent the will of God from being achieved. More than anything else, in regard to salvation, is man's free moral agency. God will not violate or override our free choice to serve Him or reject Him. All could be saved, but all will not be saved because many refuse to accept God's terms of salvation. By the same token, all could be healed, but all won't be healed because many are ignorant of how to appropriate divine healing. Either that or something is hindering their healing from manifesting.

Rest assured it is God's will to heal you. Don't let the enemy rob your inheritance as a child of God with his seeds of doubt. The Bible declares, *"No good thing will He withhold from them that walk uprightly."* (Ps. 84:11 KJV) But we must keep in mind that the blessings of God are conditional. His love is unconditional, but His blessings are often conditional upon our obedience. Friend, if you are in need of healing or a miracle, consider these suggestions carefully:

Consider the Greatness of God

When my parents believed God for a new bone in my leg, they kept reminding themselves and the Lord of

His greatness in prayer. They reasoned, if God could create 206 bones in my body when He formed me in the womb, how hard would it be for God to replace one piece of missing bone? The Bible teaches that *"nothing is too difficult"* and *"nothing is impossible"* for the Lord.

Often we categorize sicknesses in our mind in degrees of curability. We, in our finite reasoning, assume some sicknesses are easy for God to heal while other more serious illnesses are tougher. But the supernatural is natural with God. Miracles to God are like breathing to us. He doesn't exert more energy to perform a "big" miracle or less energy to work a "small" miracle. He is God Omnipotent—all powerful! Cancer is no more of a challenge to God than a cold. But our minds are conditioned by the limitations of medical science. If the doctors find certain diseases *Miracles to God are like breathing. Cancer is no more of a challenge to God than a cold.* difficult to treat and cure, then we think maybe they are harder for God to deal with too? Not so!

The God we serve is the Creator of the universe. He is so infinitely large that He inhabits eternity and yet so infinitely small that He dwells within our hearts. Jeremiah extolled the awesomeness of God with these words: *"Ah, Lord God! Behold, You have made the heavens and the earth by Your great power and outstretched arm.* **There is nothing too hard for You**...*the Great, the Mighty God, whose name is the Lord of hosts...great in counsel and mighty in work...."* (Jer. 32:17–19)

Later in this same chapter, God asks, *"Behold, I am the Lord, the God of all flesh, **is there anything too hard for me?"*** Obviously, the answer is a resounding, "NO!" There is nothing too difficult for God to do!

When my mother-in-law, Faye Bolton, was pregnant with my wife back in 1969, she developed a ten pound fibroid tumor that attached itself to her uterus. The doctor informed my father-in-law that the tumor would have to be surgically removed. He said that when the tumor was cut out, the baby (my wife, Michelle) would miscarry and pass. My father-in-law, Raymond Bolton, a Pentecostal preacher, told the doctor to do what he could do and God would do the rest. During the surgery many people prayed earnestly that the baby would survive. To the amazement of the surgical team, the baby lived and was carried full term. My wife's birth was a miracle. Of course, I believe God spared her life just for me, but I'm sort of partial on that subject.

If you or someone you love needs a miracle, don't consider the magnitude of your problem, consider the greatness of your God. For if God created all we see with the Word of His power, then what sickness or disease poses a challenge to Him? Instead of telling God how big our mountain is, we need to tell our mountain how big our God is!

Hurdle Your Hindrances

The Woman with the Issue of Blood had to press through a crowd to touch the hem of Jesus' garment. (Mk. 5:25–34) Jesus stopped everything and asked, *"who touched Me?"* The disciples thought it was an absurd question since literally dozens of people were brushing up against Him by the minute. But Jesus discerned that this wasn't just a casual touch, not just incidental contact. No, this touch was different. This was a touch mixed with faith and desperation. You see, she had exhausted all of her resources on physicians, but only grew worse. She knew Jesus was her last and only hope.

Sometimes I think we approach God too casually about the things we really need. We take a fine-if-we-do, fine-if-we-don't attitude about getting our prayers answered. Just maybe God delays His answer to see how earnest we really are about our prayers. There are many examples of people in the Bible who received answers to desperate prayers. Hannah was so desperate to have a child that when she prayed in the Temple, Eli, the High Priest at the time, thought she was drunk. (See 1 Sam. 1:9–17.) But God responded to her desperate cry and not only gave her a son but seven children. Often I think we approach God too passively. Some people's mentality is, "If God wants me to be healed, He'll just drop healing right in my lap." That's not how you got saved, is it? No, you sought aggressively after God when the Holy Spirit drew you. Healing often works on the same principle—seek and you shall find. If we are seeking for a miracle and we want God to take us seriously, we need to get desperate and take our prayers more seriously. David prayed, *"As the deer pants for the water brooks, so pants my soul for You, O God."* (Ps. 42:1) Now that's desperation! Anytime we try to receive something from God, we will face hindrances. We need to learn to hurdle those hindrances and press on in faith into God's provision.

Feed Your Faith, Starve Your Doubts

If Job had listened to his comforters and followed their advice, he probably would have never seen God's restoration. It is easy to allow fear to cause you to expect the worst instead of the best. I recall when my wife was pregnant with our son, Nathan, how so many well-meaning mothers told her horror stories about their deliveries. Very few told her about positive experiences in childbearing. Most were very negative. They told of lengthy labor, botched epidurals, complications and hospital staff goof-ups, etc. What we had to keep reminding ourselves was that *"…God has not given us a spirit of fear; but of power, and of love, and of a sound mind."* (2 Tim. 1:7) My wife ended up in labor less than five hours and had a completely healthy son with no complications. The same was true of the births of our daughter Emily and our other son, Noah. God helped us tune out the negative reports of the naysayers.

Human tendency is to readily believe a well-meaning doctor's worst-case prognosis instead of believing the promises of God. Why are we so quick to believe a bad report and so reluctant to believe a good report? Remember the story of the twelve spies Moses sent out? (See Num. 13.) Ten brought back gripes but only two brought back grapes. Which report did the multitude believe? Joshua and Caleb pleaded, *"Let us go up at once, and possess it; for we are well able to overcome it."* (Num. 13:30 KJV) But the word "giants" was all that lingered in their minds. They envisioned a bloodbath.

They believed the evil report. So God ordered them to make a U-turn back into the wilderness and they toiled on a spiritual treadmill for forty years until an entire generation of unbelievers died. Years of sorrow could have been avoided if they had only believed God's Word.

I'm not suggesting that we retreat into denial and live in a fantasy world where nothing bad ever happens. I'm simply saying that when we receive a negative report, we shouldn't accept it as the final verdict. We serve a God who can overturn the verdict of man and change circumstances in our favor. Just as an appellate court can overturn the verdict of a lower court, even so man's verdict can

> *The big difference, however, is that faith sees the positive or God's Word, while fear sees the negative.*

be overturned in the appeals court of heaven. Whenever we receive a negative report, we can appeal it to a higher court, a higher law, a higher Judge. Learn to counteract the negative news of man with the positive promises of God.

When my doctors told my parents I would never walk normally again, they were speaking from their professional experience with cases like mine. However, my parents did not accept their word as the final verdict. They stayed focused on God's promise to heal. In fact, they made a list of all the healing promises in the Bible and read them to me and to each other. They did not deny the reality of my dilemma. But neither did they allow negative reports to handicap their faith. They believed that God had a better plan for me.

I'm not advocating a sanitized version of mind-over-matter therapy. But I do believe that what we hold on to can have a great bearing on the outcome of our circumstances. Jesus told several people, *"As your faith is, so be it unto you."* What are you believing for? To a certain degree, faith and fear mean similar things— "to see." The big difference, however, is that faith sees the positive or God's Word, while fear sees the negative. So what you see in life largely depends on what you're looking for. When Jesus was walking with Jarius to heal his sick daughter, messengers met them on the way with this negative report: *"Your daughter is dead," they said. "Why bother the teacher any more?"* **Ignoring what they said**, *Jesus told the synagogue ruler, "Don't be afraid; just believe."* (Mk. 5:35–36 NIV)

Regarding miracles, there is something to be said for how we respond to bad news. Jesus, in essence, told Jarius, "Don't panic, don't accept this report as the final verdict." Jesus simply ignored the messenger's words. We would do well to do the same. Just like Job, who turned a deaf ear to the misguided advice of his friends, we should respond to bad news by saying, *"…I know that my Redeemer lives."* (Jb. 19:25) In other words, God will bring good out of this otherwise bad situation.

Pray With Persistence

The story is told that when Winston Churchill was asked what his greatest speech was, he recalled a speech during the height of World War II. At the time, Germany appeared to be poised to defeat Great Britain and the Allied Powers. When Churchill walked to the podium in the Parliament he repeated three simple but powerful words, "Never give up! Never give up! Never give up!"

This said, he turned and exited the room to a thunderous applause. Before long, the momentum of the War shifted and the Nazi regime was overthrown.

This lesson should be applied to our prayer life. We should never give up even when we get discouraged because we don't see immediate results. Jesus gave us the Parable of the Unjust Judge in Luke 18:1–8 to illustrate this point. The purpose of this parable is clear, *"...That men ought always to pray and not to faint."* A certain widow appealed to a corrupt judge to give her justice concerning an enemy. At first he ignored her. But she didn't give up and wouldn't take "no" for an answer. She became such a nuisance that he finally granted her request just to get rid of her. Jesus concludes the story by saying, *"And shall not God avenge His own elect, which cry **day and night** unto Him, though He bear long with them? I tell you that He will avenge them speedily."* (Lu. 18:7–8 KJV) In other words, if persistence pays when dealing with a crooked judge who has no interest in your case, how much more does it pay when your dealing with the just Judge of all the Earth who has a supreme interest in your case!

Some people teach that if you pray for something more than once, you are praying in unbelief. This teaching is very unscriptural. Elijah prayed seven times until he saw the cloud indicating that God had answered him (1 Kgs. 18:41–45, Ja. 5:17–18). Even Jesus prayed for a blind man twice before he was totally healed (Mk. 8:22–26) and prayed the same prayer three times in the Garden of Gethsemane (Mt. 26:44). The Apostle Paul prayed for God to remove his thorn in the flesh on three occasions (2 Cor. 12:7–9). Were these great men of God praying in unbelief because they prayed for the same thing more than once? Of course not! They knew the secret of persistence. God doesn't always answer our prayers when we want or how we want. But if we refuse to give up, our need will be met in God's time and way. Like Jacob of the Old Testament, we should adopt this attitude—"...*I will not let You go unless You bless me!*" (Gen. 32:26) This kind of tenacity and bulldog faith pleases God, provided the thing we are seeking for is His will. If we are asking for something contrary to God's will, He, in His wisdom, will withhold it from us for our own good (Ja. 4:3, 1 Jn. 5:14–15).

There are several examples in Scripture of how faith and prayer changed the mind of God. King Hezekiah, for instance, became terminally ill at age thirty-nine when a boil erupted on his body. God sent the prophet Isaiah with this solemn message, "...*Set your house in order, for you shall die, and not live.*" (2 Kgs. 20:1) You'd think that if God said something as emphatic as that, it would be final. Curtains! Case closed! Instead of accepting the message at face value, Hezekiah turned his face to the palace wall and began to weep and pray, reminding God how he had lived righteously. God was so moved by the King's sincerity that He prompted Isaiah back to the King's bedchamber. "*Return and tell Hezekiah... I have heard your prayer, I have seen your tears; surely I will heal you...And I will add to your days fifteen years....*" (2 Kgs. 20:5–6) Isaiah instructed him to place a lump of figs over the boil. Three days later, the king was restored to health and went to the Temple to worship the One who extended his life. Hezekiah's

Prayer moves the hand that moves the world!

prayer changed the mind of God. What power there is in prayer! *Prayer moves the hand that moves the world![8]*

When it comes to persistence in prayer, the secret is to ask and keep asking. Seek and keep seeking. Knock and keep knocking. Eventually, in God's time, you will receive, you will find, and the door will be opened unto you. Friend, if you need a miracle, there is hope. We serve a God who specializes in doing the impossible. A wise man once said, "Impossibilities with men are opportunities with God!" Don't give up. God hears your prayers and sees your tears. Keep fighting the good fight of faith. Your answer may be closer than you think. Meditate a few moments on the message of this hymn:

> *Got any rivers you think are uncrossable?*
> *Got any mountains you can't tunnel thru?*
> *God specializes in things tho't impossible,*
> *And He can do what no other pow'r can do.[9]*

Why God Allows Tragedy

Being a Christian doesn't guarantee trouble-free living. Even being in the perfect will of God doesn't exempt believers from all tragedy. I have heard it said that Christians are like tea bags—they're not good for much until they're in hot water! Just as hot water flushes the flavor out of tea bags, the adverse circumstances we face present opportunities for the nature of Jesus to surface in our lives. Psalm 34:19 braces us for reality by stating, *"Many are the afflictions of the righteous"* and then promises us victory by adding, *"But the Lord delivers him out of them all."* Jesus predicted that *"...In the world ye shall have tribulation...."* Then He reassured us by adding, *"But be of good cheer; I have overcome the world."* (Jn. 16:33 KJV)

It's only realistic to assume that at some point in our lives we will encounter tragedy. Consequently, we need an understanding of the reasons why God allows tragedy to carry us through those difficult times.

Keep in mind that there are many things that we simply cannot and will not understand in this realm. Some things won't be fully understood until Jesus returns. Other things we can know here and now. We should follow this important rule of thumb: where the Bible is vague, we should be vague; where the Bible is specific, we should be specific.

Human nature is inherently curious. When bad things happen to good people, we invariably want an explanation. Without question, God could prevent the tragedy that has become so common in the human experience. And yet, for many reasons, He allows it. Why? This is a question we have asked ourselves, perhaps our pastor or even God Himself. To find relevant answers to this complex question, let's use a tragic case study found in John's Gospel, chapter eleven.

"Lord, Lazarus Is Sick"

Mary, Martha and Lazarus were close friends of Jesus and are the main characters in this story. The Gospels document the mutual love that existed between the Master and this trio. Apparently, Jesus made frequent stops in Bethany to eat, lodge and fellowship with this family (Mt. 21:17, Lu. 10:38–42, Jn. 11:1–5, 35–36; 12:1–11). It is speculated that Martha was a widow who, upon her husband's death, had her younger siblings move in.[10] At any rate, Lazarus became seriously ill, insomuch that his sisters sent an urgent message to Jesus some twenty miles away. The message: *"Lord, the one You love is sick."* (Jn. 11:3 NIV) The Bible informs us that Jesus deliberately delayed for two days. But why? Could it be that He had a higher purpose in mind?

The people who gathered at the tomb of Lazarus asked, *"Could not He who opened the eyes of the blind man have kept this man from dying?"* (Jn. 11:37 NIV) The obvious answer is YES! Jesus could have easily prevented the death of Lazarus. But why didn't He? That's the question we all have. Some suggest that Jesus delayed because of a superstition many Jews of that day believed—that the spirit of a dead person hovered around the corpse for three days. This they believed because a corpse usually didn't begin to decompose until the fourth day.[11] Remember what Martha said when Jesus boldly commanded the stone to be removed from Lazarus' grave? *"Lord, by this time there is a stench, for he has been dead four days."* (Jn. 11:39 KJV) It is also believed that one of the reasons Jesus Himself arose from the dead on the third day (before decomposition began) was to fulfill this specific prophecy, *"...Nor will You allow Your Holy One to see corruption."* (Ps. 16:10 KJV)[12]

Jesus had previously raised two other people from the dead (that we have record of): Jarius' daughter (Mark 5) and the Widow's son at Nain (Luke 7). In the first case, Jarius' twelve year old girl had only been dead a matter of minutes when Jesus arrived and revived her. In the second case,

> *Sometimes God allows a small tragedy to prevent a bigger tragedy—the loss of one's soul.*

Jesus actually interrupted the funeral to bring the young man back to life. Jews were known to have swift burials so he was probably dead for no more than one or two days. Conceivably, all the critics who believed the spirit remained near the corpse for three days, discounted those resurrections as somehow invalid.

Presumably, they contended that they weren't *really* dead just "asleep" or in what we know as a coma. Of course, this is merely speculation.

So when Jesus received the news of Lazarus' illness, He simply bided His time. Perhaps He decided not only to allow Lazarus to die, but to deliberately wait until the fourth day to arrive at the tomb, knowing the body would have already begun to decompose. (See Jn. 11:39.) When Lazarus was raised from the dead, not only was he revived, but the decomposition process was reversed, proving once and for all to the superstitious skeptics that Jesus' power was real. Let's examine six major reasons God allows tragedy when, in His Sovereignty, He could prevent it:

1. To Manifest His Glory.

In Lazarus' case, Jesus explained why He allowed His dear friend to die, *"This sickness will not end in death. No, **it is for God's glory** so that God's Son may be glorified through it."* (Jn. 11:4 NIV) In other words, the only reason Jesus allowed Lazarus to die was so He could resurrect him and thus glorify Himself.

Another instance of this is located in John 9:1-7. In this passage, Jesus and His trusted Twelve passed a man who was blind from birth. The disciples asked, *"...Who did sin, this man or his parents, that he was born blind?"* Think through this question carefully. How could the man have sinned before he was born and, as punishment for that sin, be born blind? The question makes no sense unless you realize that some Jews of Jesus' day believed in a previous existence, some brand of reincarnation.[13] In essence, what the disciples are asking is "Did this man sin in a former life or state of existence in order to come into this world blind?" Jesus quickly put the question to rest. *"Neither this man nor his parents sinned,"* said Jesus, *"but this happened so that* **the work of God** *might be displayed in his life."* (Jn. 9:3 NIV) Again, the only reason the man had this birth defect was so Jesus could cure him and thereby glorify Himself.

What we learn from this story is that problems do not always indicate sin. In fact, sometimes problems are an indication that you're doing something right and the enemy is just out to get you. When things go wrong, evil spirits usually accuse us of sin. They try to convince us, as Job's miserable comforters did, that our mishaps are a result of our misdeeds. Sometimes even our own mind condemns us. The truth is, tragedy is often just an opportunity for God to manifest His glory in our lives. Remember, God can bring good out of any bad situation "And we know that in all things God works for the good of those who love him...." (Ro. 8:28 NIV) He never promised that everything that happened to us would be good; rather, He promised to bring good out of it.

> *The truth is, tragedy is often just an opportunity for God to manifest His glory in our lives.*

When this is the case in a given tragedy, the result will bring glory to God and yield a powerful testimony. After Lazarus' resurrection, Jesus later returned to Bethany for a special supper that Martha and Mary prepared for Him. When news spread that Jesus was there, a large crowd swarmed the house, not only to see Jesus but, as John 12:9–11 (NIV) records, *"...To see Lazarus whom He had raised from the dead. So the chief priests made plans to kill Lazarus as well, for on account of him many of the Jews were going over to Jesus and putting their faith in Him."* While Jesus did allow Lazarus' tragic death, look at the end result—it produced a testimony that, in turn, produced many believers. Lazarus became a living testimony, a tangible example of what God's power could do. Tragedy, to a believer, is occasionally just a trial preceding a blessing.

I want to clarify an issue to avoid misunderstanding. I strongly disagree with teaching implying that God puts sickness on His children and that their suffering somehow gives Him glory. If that were true, then we would need to pray for more sickness so God would get more glory (pardon the sarcasm). No, God does not afflict His children with tragedy but, on occasion, He does allow it. Keep in mind that Satan is the one who comes *"To steal, to kill and to destroy."* Scripture is clear that God permitted Satan to afflict Job for a season. But the devil was the one who did the afflicting, not God. So when tragedy knocks at your door, realize it may just be an opportunity for God to answer it and display His mighty power.

> *The good thing about trouble is it makes you pray.*

Incidentally, Lazarus' name means *"without help."*[14] As Christians, we will all face seemingly helpless situations from time to time. That is not negativism; it's realism. But even if you feel helpless, know that you are not hopeless! Life without Jesus is a hopeless end, but life with Jesus is endless hope! Does it seem like God is delaying an answer to your prayers as He did with Mary and Martha? Take comfort, friend, a delay does not necessarily mean a denial!

2. To Change Our Direction.

Sadly but truly, it often takes drastic measures for God to get some people's attention. Do you recall the story of King Nebuchadnezzar in Daniel, chapter four? Because of his arrogance and hardness of heart, God allowed a terrifying tragedy to bring him to his knees. God even warned the potentate through a dream about a massive tree that produced shade and shelter for much of the animal kingdom. Daniel interpreted the tree to represent Nebuchadnezzar and the Babylonian Empire God enabled him to build. Then, in the dream, the tree was cut down, leaving only the stump. This, according to Daniel, was God's ultimatum, that if the King didn't humble himself, his kingdom would be removed. Still, Nebuchadnezzar remained absorbed in his own self-importance.

One year after Daniel implored him to repent, the King strolled on the balcony of his palace, boasting of the great City of Babylon he had built. Suddenly, a voice from heaven thundered, *"The kingdom has departed from you."* (Dan. 4:31) He was stricken with lycanthropy—a mental disorder that causes people to imagine themselves as an animal. For seven *"times"* (probably either months or years) he remained in this deranged state. He ate grass like an ox, his hair grew out like eagle's feathers and his fingernails and toenails grew out like a hawk's talons. Eventually restored to his senses, the king humbled himself and exalted God as the King of all the earth.

Sometimes God allows a small tragedy to prevent a bigger tragedy—the loss of one's soul. Jesus taught that it is far better to enter into heaven handicapped than to enter hell healthy (Mt. 18:8–9). Certain people have confided to me that if certain tragedies had not occurred to them, they probably would have never gotten saved, they probably would have died young due to their lifestyle and ended up lost eternally.

One of my own brothers, Jesse, rebelled against God and our parents as a teenager. After running away from home at sixteen, he began using and selling drugs. He was arrested for selling drugs and faced three drug-related charges carrying fifteen-year, five-year and three-year prison sentences. The minimum mandatory sentence was five years in the Florida State Penitentiary. It was only when his life hit a dead end that he turned to God and was gloriously saved. He has since completed Bible College and has been involved in ministry. He would tell you that, but for his tragedy, he might not be serving God today. His life was revolutionized and, as a result of prayer, his sentence was reduced to five years of probation, of which he only served two and one-half years due to excellent behavior.

Saul's testimony further illustrates how God can use tragedy to change a person's direction. Acts, chapter nine, records how Saul was traveling to Damascus to imprison, persecute and, possibly, execute believers. Then Jesus appeared in a blinding light and revealed Himself to him as the true Messiah. Saul, a student of Gamaliel and a Pharisee, knew all about the Jewish religion but he didn't know Jesus. As a result, Saul was blinded for three days until Ananias prayed for him. When he received his sight and the gift of the Holy Spirit, his name and his life's direction were changed. He later became the mighty Apostle Paul who contributed either thirteen or fourteen books of the New Testament (depending on whether or not he authored Hebrews).

So you see, God can use tragedy to change people's direction. Some people are so stubborn and hard-hearted that it takes a tragedy for them to hit the altar which, in turn, alters the course of their life.

3. To Draw Us Closer To Himself.

Many people treat God like the paramedics—they only call when they have an emergency! All teasing aside, there is nothing like hard times that will help us see our need to pray. Sometimes I read with envy the passionate words of the Psalmist David as he graphically details his quest for God. He comes across so spiritual and so single-minded. Here is a sampling:

- *"As the deer pants for the water brooks, so pants my soul for You, O God."* (Ps. 42:1)

- *"One thing I have desired of the Lord, that will I seek: that I may dwell in the house of the Lord all the days of my life, to behold the beauty of the Lord, and to inquire in His temple."* (Ps. 27:4)

- *"Let the words of my mouth and the meditation of my heart, be acceptable in Your sight, O Lord, my Strength, and my Redeemer."* (Ps. 19:14)

- *"Create in me a clean heart, O God; and renew the right spirit within me."* (Ps. 51:10 KJV)

- *"Whom have I in heaven but You? and there is none upon earth I desire beside You."* (Ps. 73:25)

Reading words like these can give you a complex and leave you feeling inferior, like a spiritual dwarf by comparison. They seem so pious and devout. But have you ever wondered what made David a man after God's own heart? What drove him to the point where all he wanted was God? The answer, in a word, is *trouble*! It was the unbelievable calamity, persecution and hardship David faced that drove him to an intimate walk with God. David got to the point where all he wanted was more of God, because so many other things in his life brought bitter disappointment.

Think about it. His brothers rejected him and questioned his motives when he offered to fight Goliath. King Saul mounted a massive manhunt and chased him like a fugitive for years. His first wife, Merab, King Saul's daughter, was given to another man. Another wife, Michael, despised him in her heart. Later on in his life his daughter, Tamar, was raped by his son, Amnon. Absalom, another of David's sons, in turn, murdered Amnon for violating Tamar. Absalom later plotted a coup against David's throne. All of this not to mention his own adultery with Bathsheba and the subsequent cover up and murder of her husband, Uriah the Hittite. Plus, on top of all this, there was the death of their illegitimate child. Perhaps the real reason David became a man after God's own heart was because so many things in his life broke his heart. The point is that trouble will either drive us farther away or closer to God. It is evident by the following lyrics that David had more than his share of tragedy:

> "This poor man cried, and the Lord heard him, and saved him out of all his troubles." (Ps. 34:6 KJV)

> "The righteous cry out, and the Lord hears, and delivers them out of all their troubles." (Ps. 34:17)

- *"Even my own familiar friend in whom I trusted, who ate my bread, has lifted up his heel against me."* (Ps. 41:9)

- *"As with a breaking of my bones, my enemies reproach me, while they say to me all day long, 'Where is your God?'"* (Ps. 42:10)

- *"Lord, how are they increased that trouble me! many are they that rise up against me. Many there be which say of my soul, there is no help for him in God."* (Ps. 3:1–2 KJV)

Tragedy has a way of reminding us just how fragile life really is. It is in those times that we realize how much we need God. I have read and heard about the great revivals of the late 1940's and early 1950's. There was such a sovereign move of God across America. Literally hundreds of thousands of people were saved, healed and delivered in the giant tent crusades conducted by men like Oral Roberts, William Branham, A. A. Allen, R. W. Shambach, Jack Coe and a host of others. I've often wondered why that particular period was so spiritually prosperous? Then it occurred to me that it was during the post World War II era. Families had been ravaged by the loss or injury of loved ones. The whole world witnessed the evil of Hitler's regime. Medical science was still inexact by today's standards. Our nation was exhausted by the physical, emotional and economical toll of the war. America was ripe for revival!

As a nation, we knew we needed God. We knew that without God's intervention the Allied Powers could have been defeated. With a simple turn of fate, Germany could have become the dominant global power. (Imagine living under the tyranny of Nazism.) Our trust was not in money or technology since, for the most part, people didn't have a whole lot of either. Our national trust was in God during the post-war rebuilding. There was a strong connection between people's hunger for God at that time and the great revivals that resulted. After the tragedies of war, America was collectively drawn closer to God as revival winds swept across this country.

Today, with all of the anti-God, anti-Bible, anti-prayer and anti-morality sentiment in our nation, still all it takes is a major national tragedy (like the World Trade Center terrorist attack or Hurricane Katrina) for America to find its way back to its knees. You see, nothing like trouble makes us pray. That is the one good thing about hard times—they make you pray more! So, sometimes, God allows tragedy in order to draw us closer to Himself. What we must learn to do is make God our first resource, not our last resort.

4. To Prepare Us For Specific Ministry.

In Luke 22:31–32, Jesus predicted that Peter would go through a difficult spiritual process called sifting. He warned Peter that Satan would try to sift him like wheat. Sifting, though unpleasant at times, is actually a good process. God and Satan, however, sift us with two opposite motives in mind: God sifts us to separate the wheat from the chaff (spiritual from carnal); Satan sifts us with the intention of destroying the wheat (the regenerated part of us). Jesus added this instruction to Peter, *"When you are converted, strengthen thy brethren."* In other words, Jesus was saying, "I'm going to let you go through some things for the purpose of preparing you to minister to others." Sometimes God allows tragedy for this reason.

Take an alcoholic, for instance. I have met many people who tragically wasted many years, not to mention a small fortune, consuming liquor. These individuals are now saved, serving God and some are in ministry. Why did God let them go through that? Part of it, of course, was their own choosing. Certainly it wasn't God's will for them, but He can use that as a means of ministering to others who are caught in the same trap. If I was addicted to alcohol, I'd want to go to someone for counsel and prayer who had been there and who knew what I was going through. The

> *Every tragedy can present an opportunity for ministry. First we receive it, then we give it.*

same could be said for drugs, cigarettes, gambling and other addictive behaviors. See, once you've been through something yourself, you can relate with compassion to those who are struggling with it. In the event of a miscarriage or the loss of a loved one, it's comforting to talk with someone who has been there before and who knows how you feel. So every tragedy can present an opportunity for ministry. First we receive it, then we give it.

A missionary that our church has supported for many years, Jack Kinley, was blown out of a tank during World War II. The three other soldiers who were with him in the tank were instantly killed. He alone survived. After a temporary loss of both hearing and sight, he recovered and was sent back into service. As time passed, his eyesight gradually diminished. Doctors discovered that the concussion he sustained during the tank bombing had irreparably damaged his optic nerve. Today, he can only decipher light and dark in one eye. Still, with this physical limitation, Bro. Kinley travels overseas preaching, distributing literature and taking the Bible on cassette with tape players to the visually impaired. God has used him to win hundreds of souls. This tragedy occurred before he was saved, but God spared his life and, even though he lost his sight, God has used it as an open door of ministry to people with a similar problem. This shows you how God can take a negative and make it a positive for His glory. If you have had a tragedy, seek the Lord for divinely inspired ideas on how you can turn it into an opportunity to minister to others.

5. To Bring Correction.

In John, chapter five, we read of an invalid man whose infirmity left him bedridden for thirty-eight grueling years. Jesus healed him and sent him on his way walking under his own power. Later, Jesus found him in the temple and gave him this stern warning, *"See, you have been made well. Sin no more, lest a worse thing come upon you."* (Jn. 5:14) This statement seems to indicate that this sickness was a direct result of the man's sin. While this is not true in every case, occasionally sin is the direct culprit for a tragedy. In fact, some tragedies people bring on themselves by violating God's moral laws or abusing their bodies. For instance, sexually transmitted diseases, lung cancer and cirrhosis of the liver are often self-inflicted by promiscuity, smoking and alcohol consumption respectively. Numerous other diseases are caused by unhealthy diets. It is counter productive to pray for God to heal us of problems while all along we are contributing to the cause.

Do we honestly believe that God will remove physical or spiritual problems that our habits, behavior or diets are actually causing? Who do we think we're fooling?

Too often even Christians are guilty of creating messes and expecting God to bail them out. Excessive debt is one good example. Sure, God has promised to supply all of our needs, but He never promised to finance all of our wants. God can certainly supply supernaturally but He also expects us to use wisdom and common sense and be good stewards of His resources. Some believers have quit tithing because, after doing it faithfully for years, they've gotten into a financial bind and presume that God has let them down. More often than not, they simply overextended themselves into debt and are now reaping the consequences. God didn't let them down; they let themselves down! We must repent and change our ways before we can legitimately expect God to intervene. I'm convinced that when God told the Children of Israel *"...I will put none of the diseases on you which I have brought on the Egyptians. For I am the Lord who heals you"* (Ex. 15:26), He fully expected them to pay heed to His dietary laws. And, while we are certainly not under bondage to the dietary laws of the Old Testament (Ac. 10:9–16, Ro. 14:17), it still makes sense that God, who wisely designed the human body, knows what is and isn't good for it. He gave those laws with our best interest at heart. Simple common sense and self-restraint could literally add years to our lives.

If God allows tragedy for the purpose of correction, it is never intended to destroy us but to restore us to fellowship with Himself (Heb. 12:5–11). James 5:14 instructs us to call for the elders of the church to anoint and pray for us in the event of sickness. Verse fifteen continues by saying, *"And the prayer of faith will save the sick, and the Lord will raise him up. And if he has committed sins, he will be forgiven."* In other words, if the sickness is a result of sin, not only will God heal the sickness but He will also forgive the sin that caused the sickness, provided we repent.

God doesn't enjoy correcting his children any more than an earthly parent does. But, in His unconditional love for us, He will not allow us to continue in behavior that is detrimental to our spiritual or physical welfare. *"My son, do not despise the chastening of the Lord, nor be discouraged when you are rebuked by Him; for whom the Lord loves He chastens, and scourges every son whom He receives."* (Heb. 12:5–6) In my opinion, chastisement can take the form of a sickness, a financial crisis, a family conflict or any number of other problems. I don't believe that God is the one who afflicts believers with these things, but our disobedience can certainly open the door to these intruders. There are numerous instances in the Bible where God used Israel's enemies to chastise His own people in order to bring them to repentance. God's purpose is always restoration, not destruction, and He is much fairer than human parents. His correction is always tempered with mercy. True love, you see, doesn't allow someone to persist in self-destructive behavior. Love doesn't stand by and watch a person do what they want when it is harmful to them or to others. Love actually has two sides: a tough side and a tender side.[15] God knows how to administer the perfect balance of both—the tender when we need His gentle reassurance, the tough when we need His firm correction.

David captured this concept in the Shepherd Psalm (Psalm 23) when he said of the Good Shepherd, *"... Your* **rod** *and Your* **staff***, they comfort me."* A shepherd in Bible times carried a staff with a crook on it to retrieve a wandering sheep from a thicket or a perilous ledge. He also used a rod to fend off wolves or to actually break the hind leg of a habitually wayward sheep. It was for the sheep's own good. Too many dangers lurked outside the safety of the flock. After breaking the lamb's leg, the shepherd would gently nurse it back to health and even carry it on his shoulders. What a powerful portrait of the Father's loving care for us. Thank God that He loves us enough to discipline us when we need it. Jesus, the Good Shepherd, gives us what we need, not just what we want. Perhaps that is why the Psalmist wrote, *"He* **makes** *me to lie down in green pastures...."* (Ps. 23:2)

The principle here is short-term pain in exchange for long-term gain. Surgery is never pleasant but often necessary for our long-term good. Whenever we undergo the scalpel of God's Word, we must realize that He always knows what is best for us and He has our best interest in mind. He also knows how and when to prune our tree to ensure maximum fruit bearing (Jn. 15:2).

6. A Fallen World System.

We live in a fallen world system. This world does not function like God originally intended for it to function. The early chapters of Genesis describe the beauty and harmony that existed in nature and creation prior to the fall. Abruptly, sin intruded, turning order into chaos. Thorns and thistles erupted from the ground. Man became aware of his nakedness. Animals that co-existed in perfect harmony were transformed into beastly predators and wary prey. The first blood was spilled as the survival of the fittest began. The pungent smell of death polluted the air. The whimpering of the wounded sent shock waves of fear to the survivors.

We have not only inherited a fallen nature, we have inherited a fallen world. When Adam fell, creation itself was dealt a devastating blow. God never intended for there to be death, sin, disease, divorce, crime, poverty, injustice, prejudice, etc. These things are all results of the fall. None of these were in God's original blueprint for mankind. But, because of man's sin, all of these negative factors have become a part of the human experience.

> *We have not only inherited a fallen nature, we have inherited a fallen world.*

I don't pretend to have all the answers. But part of the problem is we have finite minds and we are trying to comprehend infinite truth. God has a much higher perspective on these things. That's why we must learn to trust Him. Many questions we simply cannot answer. They simply defy reasoning. For instance, we don't understand why life-long Christians die with cancer. What about missionaries who are martyred? Or evangelists who perish in plane crashes? Or ministers who have heart attacks? What about the innocent children who are born with crippling birth defects? The list goes on and on. Stillbirths? Miscarriages? What about the godly people that are randomly killed in car accidents, hurricanes, tornadoes, earthquakes, floods, fires, explosions, etc? Some things are just beyond our ability to comprehend. Some things render words meaningless and empty. Some things are so unfathomable that they cannot be contained in our neat, tidy theological boxes.

While we don't have answers that specifically apply to every case of tragedy, we do know that we live in an imperfect world. Jesus offered this sobering reality check: *"...for He makes His sun rise on the evil and on the good, and sends rain on the just and on the unjust."* (Mt. 5:45) Contrary to popular theology, Christians aren't guaranteed exemption from all tragedy. Some of the tragedies we face are merely a result of living in a fallen world.

Well, there you have it—six of the major reasons why God allows tragedy. Of course, you could add several more reasons to this list. And there are many unanswered questions about cases that don't necessarily fit into any of these categories. But hopefully you have a better understanding of why some tragedies occur. Let's take another look at the six major reasons God allows tragedy that we've discussed.

"Adversity is God's university!"

1. To Manifest His Glory.

2. To Change Our Direction.

3. To Draw Us Closer to Himself.

4. To Prepare Us for Specific Ministry.

5. To Bring Correction.

6. A Fallen World System.

If you, as I do, wrestle with the unsolved mysteries associated with tragedy, perhaps the lyrics of the following song will be meaningful:

Why?

They say that into every life some rain must fall
For the pain is no respecter of the mighty or the small
But sometimes it just seems so unfair
To see the one who's had more than his share
Oh it makes you wonder why

And Lord I wouldn't second guess Your mighty plan
For I know You have a purpose
That's beyond the scope of man
If You look inside my heart You will find
That I have always been the trusting kind
Oh but still I wonder

Why do the rainy days have to come
When the storm clouds hide the sun
I want to know why
Why when the reasons aren't clear to me
When it all is a mystery
I want to know why
And though down here I may not understand
I won't let go of the unseen hand…
For it holds the reasons why.[16]

Beauty For Ashes

Once again, God never promised everything that happens in our lives will be good. But we must have faith that He can produce good out of it. Long before Jesus came, Isaiah prophesied in graphic detail what His ministry would accomplish:

*"The Spirit of the Lord God is upon Me; because the Lord hath anointed Me to preach good tidings to the meek; He hath sent me to bind up the broken hearted, to proclaim liberty to the captives, and the opening of the prison to them that are bound; to proclaim the acceptable year of the Lord, and the day of vengeance of our God; to comfort all that mourn; to appoint unto them that mourn in Zion, to give unto them **beauty for ashes**, the garment of praise for the spirit of heaviness; that they might be called trees of righteousness, the planting of the Lord, that He might be glorified."* (Is. 61:1–3 KJV)

Over 700 years later, Jesus stood up in the crowded synagogue in Nazareth and announced that this prophecy was being fulfilled right before their eyes (Lu. 4:16–21).

Notice the pleasantly powerful phrase *"beauty for ashes."* In Bible times, people either sat in ashes or placed them upon their heads during times of mourning, grief or repentance. There are several instances in Scripture in which ashes were used to symbolize and express profound grief. Tamar, for example, put ashes on her head in grief after being raped by her half brother Amnon (2 Sam. 13:19). When Job's ten children were killed in a tornado-like storm and his body erupted with sore boils, he mourned in ashes (Jb. 1:19–20; 2:7–8). Later he sat in dust and ashes as a method of humbling himself in repentance before God (Jb. 42:6). Furthermore, when Mordecai heard the news in Babylon of Haman's sinister plot of genocide against the Jews, he wept in sackcloth and ashes along with his fellow countrymen (Es. 4:1–3). Daniel also sought God in this manner to gain understanding of the visions the Lord showed him (Dan. 9:3). The King of Nineveh repented in similar fashion after hearing the preaching of Jonah and commanded his subjects to do likewise or suffer the penalty of death (Jo. 3:4–9). As you can tell, ashes were used as a universal symbol for sorrow.

The powerful truth Isaiah prophesied is that Jesus would come to give us "beauty for ashes." By "beauty", the prophet is referring to something else that was placed on people's heads at times of celebration. The New International Version renders it, *"A crown of beauty."* It is a reference to a garland crown that was used for celebrations (i.e. weddings, holidays, feasts, etc.) The interpretation is that God can and will take the things that cause us sorrow and pain and turn them into a source of joy and victory.

A New Beginning

Many times when something devastating occurs in our lives we tend to think of it as being a bitter end. But disaster, while difficult to endure, can be a new beginning if we face it with the right attitude. The story is told about the burning of Thomas Edison's laboratory in 1914. The damage exceeded two million dollars, while the buildings were only insured for $238,000.00 A good portion of Edison's life's work went up in smoke that December night.

As flames engulfed the buildings, Edison's twenty-four year old son, Charles, found his father calmly watching the spectacle. "My heart ached for him," said Charles. "He was sixty-seven—no longer a young man—and everything was going up in flames. When he saw me, he shouted, 'Charles, where's your mother?' When I told him I didn't know, he said, 'Find her. Bring her here. She will never see anything like this as long as she lives.'" Apparently, the chemicals and other components to his experiments on his inventions produced a dazzling fireworks display.

The following day, Edison searched the ruins for anything salvageable and said, "There is great value in disaster. All our mistakes are burned up. Thank God we can start anew." Instead of allowing the tragedy to force him into retirement, Edison produced his first phonograph only three weeks later.[17]

Amazingly, Thomas Edison only received three months of formal education and was thought by his teachers to be slow and unteachable. He was home schooled by his mother, a former teacher. He also endured a deaf condition which he thought was caused by being lifted by the ears onto a moving train as a boy but was probably the result of having scarlet fever when he was young. In all, Edison acquired more than 1300 U.S. and foreign patents on his inventions.[18]

> *There is great value in disaster. All our mistakes are burned up. Thank God we can start anew.*

As you can see, tragedy doesn't have to be a bitter end. It can be a new beginning depending on how you react to it. A wise man once wrote, "Adversity is God's university!"[19] We can either let tragedy destroy us or we can learn and grow from it. The choice is ours.

God Knows Your Limits

It is comforting to know that no matter what we face in life, God is aware of it, and is sensitive to our pain. He is our constant companion. He will go with us through every trial. The Psalmist gave us a glimpse of the father heart of God with these words: *"As a father pities his children, So the Lord pities those who fear Him. For He knows our frame; He remembers that we are dust."* (Ps. 103:13–14) God knows our frame. He knows our limitations. He also knows how much we can handle and He promised not to put on us more than we can bear. 1 Corinthians 10:13 gives this assurance: *"No temptation* [trial] *has overtaken you except such as is common to man; but God is faithful, who will not allow you to be tempted* [tested] ***beyond what you are able....***"

Sometimes we feel so isolated, like we are the only ones going through severe problems. This verse informs us that what we are facing is *"common to man."* In other words, there are other people who are going through very similar situations, perhaps even worse. You're not the only one.

I recall reading a compelling story about a fifteen year old boy, named Chris, who was in a tragic car accident with five of his friends in Connecticut. Their car spun out of control when it hit a patch of ice and slammed into a guardrail. Three of the teens, Chris included, were hurled out of the car. One of them was killed instantly. Another was seriously injured. Chris' left leg was severed at the knee by a guardrail cable and was lying on the ground about twenty feet from his writhing body.

Chris, a star junior-high basketball player, was from a strong Christian family. When doctors informed them that his leg could not be reattached, they were understandably devastated. It seemed like his days of playing basketball were over.

But this young man was determined to play again. Months of therapy on an artificial limb ensued. At first, Chris maneuvered very clumsily, lost his balance and frequently fell. But, gradually, he gained coordination. He worked hard during the off season. His goal the following year was to make the basketball team. But he didn't want to get on the roster due to sympathy, he wanted to earn a spot.

Just eight days shy of the one-year anniversary of his accident, Chris returned to the court to play for his school. What he lacked in agility, he made up for in effort. When the final buzzer sounded, Chris had scored eleven points and his team had won the game. Chris' mother fondly relayed a story about a day she drove him home from therapy not long after his accident. Staring out the car window, Chris said, "Mom, I know why this happened to me." His mother listened intently for his next words. "God knew I could handle it, He saved my life because He knew I could handle it."[20]

"I know why this happened to me, God knew I could handle it."

Friend, let me assure you, God knows how much you can handle. He will not put upon you more than you can bear although, at times, it may feel like you're sinking beneath the load. Mother Theresa once said something like, "I know God promised not to put more on me than I can handle, but sometimes I wonder why He has so much confidence in me." It may seem like God has abandoned you or that your prayers are being ignored. You may feel like Mary and Martha did when it was time for Lazarus' funeral to begin and Jesus was nowhere in sight. How lonely they must have felt! I encourage you to give your ashes to God. Your disappointments, sorrows, failures, heartaches—give them all to your heavenly Father because He can give you beauty for ashes. He can take the things that have caused you grief and pain and produce a testimony that will bring you joy and victory. In the words of Bill Gaither's timeless classic:

"Give them all, give them all, give them all to Jesus,
Shattered dreams, wounded hearts, broken toys.
Give them all, give them all, give them all to Jesus,
And He will turn your sorrows into joy."

I'm sure you will recognize the following poem popularly known as *Footprints*. I want to close this chapter with it because it conveys the comforting message that Jesus really is nearer to us than we think. When you think He is nowhere to be found, He's just as close as a prayer. Don't allow your tragedies to drive you into feelings of isolation from God because *"...Underneath are the everlasting arms...."* (Dt. 33:27 KJV) There really is a strategy behind tragedy. We are not just hapless victims of circumstance. God is in control despite any evidence to the contrary. And He has our best interest at heart. Psalm 46:1 reminds us that, *"God is our refuge and strength, **a very present help in trouble**."* God is not farther away from us when we're in trouble, rather, He is nearer to us than at any other time. He desires to turn our ashes into something beautiful.

Footprints

One night a man had a dream.
He dreamed he was walking along
the beach with the Lord.
Across the sky flashed scenes from his life.
For each scene, he noticed two sets
of footprints in the sand:
one belonged to him,
and the other to the Lord.

When the last scene of his life flashed
before him, he looked back at the footprints
in the sand. He noticed that many times
along the path of his life
there was only one set of footprints.
He also noticed that it happened
at the very lowest
and saddest times in his life.

This really bothered him
and he asked the Lord about it.
"Lord, you said that once I decided to follow you,
you'd walk with me all the way.
But I have noticed that during the
most troublesome times in my life,
there is only one set of footprints.

I don't understand why when
I needed you most you would leave me."
The Lord replied, "My precious child,
I love you and I would never leave you.
During your times of trial and suffering,
when you see only one set of footprints
it was then that I carried you."

(Author unknown)

Our Response To Tragedy

We have considered some of the reasons why God allows tragedy. Hopefully, we have at least partially answered the age-old question, "Why do bad things happen to good people?" But keep in mind that there are some things we will not be able to understand here in this life. That's why Paul wrote, *"We can see and understand only a little about God now, as if we were peering at His reflection in a poor mirror, but someday we are going to see Him in His completeness, face to face."* (1 Cor. 13:12 Tay) The same verse in another translation reads, *"At present all I know is a little fraction of the truth, but the time will come when I shall know it as fully as God knows me."* (1 Cor. 13:12 Phi) In other words, when we get to heaven all of the unanswered questions here in this life will finally be resolved once and for all. And it probably won't happen like we imagine.

I've heard many people say that when they get to heaven, they plan to have a long talk with Adam and Eve about why they partook of the forbidden fruit and caused so much sorrow for the rest of us. If the truth be known, had Adam and Eve not partaken of that fruit, one of their offspring probably would have. Others, in jest, have said they are going to ask God a list of questions about the injustices of this world and the seeming contradictions between what the Bible says and the reality of life. I seriously doubt it will happen that way. I have a feeling that once we are in the awesome presence of God and have the full mind of Christ, we will just *know*. The words of an old, familiar hymn come to mind:

"Here temptation's hidden snare often takes us unaware,
And our hearts are made to bleed
by some tho'tless word or deed;
And we wonder why the test when we try to do our best,
But will understand it better by and by.

By and by, when the morning comes,
All the saints of God are gathered home,
We'll tell the story how we overcame,
And we'll understand it better by and by."[21]

The lyrics of a more contemporary song convey a similar message:

And the pain falls like a curtain
On the things I once called certain
And I have to say the words I fear the most
I just don't know.

And the questions without answer
Come and paralyze the dancer
So I stand here on the stage afraid to move
Afraid to fall, oh, but fall I must
On this truth that my life has been formed from the dust.

God is God and I am not
I can only see a part of the picture He's painting
God is God and I am man
So I'll never understand it all
For only God is God.[22]

In the meantime, the thing that is more important than why God allows tragedy is how we respond to it. I've heard it said that two people can face very similar circumstances in life; one can be destroyed by it, the other can be made better by it. This leads me to believe that it is not what we face in life that determines what

> *It is not what we face in life that determines what we are, but how we react to what we face in life.*

we are, but how we react to what we face in life. Let's examine three common responses people have toward tragedy. All three of these can be identified by the way Mary and Martha responded to the death of their beloved brother Lazarus.

Response #1. Blame God

Remember, when Jesus heard of Lazarus' illness, He deliberately delayed for two days. (Jn. 11:6) As soon as Martha heard that Jesus was coming, she ran to meet him. She was understandably disappointed that Jesus had not come sooner. She knew Jesus could have prevented the death of her only brother. Overwhelmed by grief, and perhaps even anger, Martha said, *"Lord...if You had been here, my brother would not have died."* (Jn. 11:21 NIV) Do you sense the tone in her words? If you read between the lines, she seems to be asking, "What took You so long? Why did You wait until it was too late? Why didn't You do something about this sooner?" Martha did what many people do today—she blamed God for her misfortunes. She felt betrayed by Jesus.

Unfortunately, teaching that is out of balance with God's Word fosters this response. Truth can be taken to such an extreme that it becomes heresy. Some teaching is so unrealistic that it breeds a sense of entitlement. The Bible is very clear about God's desire and willingness to bless His people. But that doesn't mean things are always going to go our way. At times theology can get so warped that people forget who is God. We don't have the right nor the power to manipulate or order God around. Yet some people live with the attitude that God owes them something. Like Martha, if we are not careful, we can develop a sense of "I deserve better than this." The truth is if we got what we really deserve, we would be in trouble.

Job had the opportunity to blame God for his numerous calamities, but he refused to, even when his own wife recommended it. After losing ten children, 500 cows, 500 donkeys, 700 sheep, 300 camels, countless servants and his own health, he worshipped God instead of blaming Him. (Jb. 1:20) Consider Job's response to tragedy: *"...Naked I came from my mother's womb, And naked shall I return there. The Lord gave, and the Lord has taken away; Blessed be the name of the Lord. In all this Job did not sin nor charge God with wrong."* (Jb. 1:21–22) Notice that Job didn't credit the devil for his dilemma, even though he was the true culprit. Instead, Job recognized that God was in control of his fate. He knew Satan could only go as far as God allowed him. Satan, dissatisfied with Job's response, challenged God to test Job even further, *"…Skin for skin! Yes, all that a man has he will give for his life. But stretch out Your hand now, and touch his bone and his flesh, and he will surely curse You to Your face!"* (Jb. 2:4–5) So God granted Satan permission to afflict Job's body. Sore boils erupted on his skin from head to toe. He scraped his scabs with a piece of pottery until his friends couldn't even recognize him. His wife finally had enough. She encouraged him to curse God and die. She was basically asking, "How can you keep serving a God who treats you like this?" Here's Job's response: *"…You are talking like a foolish woman. Shall we accept good from God and not trouble? In all this, Job did not sin in what he said."* (Jb. 2:9–10 NIV) If we are eager to accept the blessings of God then shouldn't we also be willing to bear hardships without blaming God?

I realize that many Bible teachers would quickly point out that Job was an Old Testament figure. They might add that, under the New Covenant, Satan doesn't have the access to God that he did in Job's time. Furthermore, they might contend that Satan doesn't have the liberty to afflict believers as he did with Job. While there is some validity to those claims, take a look around. How many good people do you know who are suffering from a serious illness? My point is that sometimes what we believe is unrealistic. In no way do I underestimate God's power to heal. In fact, my life has experienced a series of miracles and a miracle is the reason for this book in the first place. But God, in His Sovereignty and by His choosing, doesn't heal everyone and doesn't always prevent tragedy. So whether a Christian can be afflicted like Job under the New Testament is debatable. But, setting his affliction aside, let me emphasize his response to it. He refused to blame God. He recognized who was the Creator and who was the creation.

A historical figure in the field of science named Ptolemy illustrates my point. Ptolemy was a second century geographer and astronomer. He erroneously believed that the earth was the center of the solar system and that the sun, stars and planets revolved around it. This school of thought prevailed until the seventeenth century when new discoveries proved it false.[23] Of course, the true order of our solar system, is that the sun is the center and the planets and the stars revolve around it. Some contemporary theology is similarly inverted. Some humanistic doctrines wrongly exalt man (even redeemed man) as the center of everything, to the extent that God exists to revolve around meeting our needs. The Bible clearly states that man was created for God's pleasure (Rev. 4:11). The very purpose man exists is to serve God, not vice versa.

The whole episode of the golden calf at Mount Sinai was over this very issue. The golden calf Aaron fashioned was actually an ox—a beast of burden—an animal that serves and works for you. So when the children of Israel bowed down to and danced before the calf in worship, more than just idolatry was at stake. They were saying by their actions, "We don't want a God we have to serve, we want a god who will serve us." Too much of modern theology conveys the same perverted message. Instead of reaffirming our faith to serve God no matter what, popular teaching misleads us to believe that God will cater to our every whim. But God should not be viewed as a Santa Claus who automatically grants our every wish. Many people today are backslidden and out of church because something bad happened in their lives and they are pointing the finger at God for it. Don't make that mistake, friend! I know many other people who have experienced terrible tragedy yet are still serving God with all their hearts. There is an elderly couple in

When we can't trace God's hand, we must learn to trust His heart.

our church who have buried two of their sons prematurely due to two separate, fatal car accidents. Yet their faith has remained unshakably strong despite this seeming injustice. You see, it's not what we face in life, but how we respond to it. God is not to blame for the sorrow in this world. He created a perfect world that was then contaminated by sin. Sin, whether directly or indirectly, is the real source of man's sorrows.

So if tragedy strikes and you feel betrayed and abandoned by God, resist the urge to blame Him. That's precisely what the devil wants you to do. Remember, God is on your side! He is the source of good things, not evil things. When we can't trace God's hand, we must learn to trust His heart. He knows what you're going through. Scripture teaches that God is most sensitive to the suffering of His children (Heb. 4:15). Even though, at times, it feels like God is nowhere to be found, when you hurt, He hurts. You are the apple of His eye. And in your hour of greatest trial, His grace is sufficient for you. He may not change your unfavorable circumstance for the better immediately, but He may desire to change your attitude toward it. In any event, He will carry you through. Trust Him, don't blame Him.

Stay In The House

Let's take a look at two Bible stories that illustrate the importance of staying in the will of God and under the canopy of His protection. First, consider the story of Passover found in Exodus 12. The tenth and final plague God sent on Egypt was a death angel that went through the land at midnight to kill the firstborn child of every Egyptian family. God instructed Moses to have each Jewish household slay a lamb and apply its blood to their door posts as a token. God had promised, *"...And when I see the blood I will **pass over** you...."* (Ex. 12:13 KJV) Then God gave this specific order: *"...And none of you shall go out at the door of his house until the morning."* (Ex. 12:22 KJV) In other words, God was saying, "Stay in the house. Stay under the protection and the covering of the blood." If a Jew would have ventured outside his house that fateful night, he would have put himself at risk by exposing himself to the judgment of God. As long as they stayed in the house, they had the guarantee of God's protection from that plague. The next morning, weeping and wailing rudely awakened Egypt out of its slumber, *"For there was not a house where there was not one dead."* (Ex. 12:30 KJV) In the land of Goshen, not one soul perished in Israel's camp. Why? They stayed in the house!

Rahab's Rehab

The second, very similar story is found in Joshua, chapters two and six. Joshua sent two spies on a reconnaissance mission to Jericho. Rahab, the harlot, probably ran an inn where she entertained her guests in more ways than one. Rahab cleverly hid the spies under stalks of flax on her roof and misdirected the King's soldiers to the countryside to search for them. Rahab told the spies that the inhabitants of Jericho heard about how God had parted the Red Sea and destroyed two kings of the Amorites in their behalf. The citizens of Jericho sensed that they were next on God's hit list. She only asked that they return her favor with a favor—that her family would be spared. They promised that her household would be spared if she displayed the scarlet rope in her window that she let them out of the city with (Rahab's house, situated on the city wall, provided direct access to and from the city). The spies added two other stipulations: (1.) That she not utter any of their business to anyone or the oath would be nullified—Js. 2:20 (2.) That all of her family remain inside her house until after the city was destroyed—Js. 2:18. Otherwise, they warned, *"...If anyone goes outside your house into the street, his blood will be on his own head; we will not be responsible...."* (Js. 2:19 NIV)

The message was the same as it was on Passover— "stay in the house." The scarlet cord in Rahab's window was a type of the blood of Jesus. The lesson we learn from both stories is clear: underneath the canopy of the blood of Jesus there is protection. Incidentally, after Jericho fell, Rahab renounced her harlotry, began traveling with Israel and later married one of the spies she helped, Salmon. And, in one of the most remarkable stories of God's grace, Rahab was included in the lineage of Jesus (Mt. 1:5), the heroes of the faith (Heb. 11:31) and became the great, great-grandmother of King David (Ru. 4:21–22). She was also cited as an example of how works compliment faith in justification (Ja. 2:25–26).

My point is that if we get out of God's will and bad things happen to us, it's not God's fault. Many people blame God for things they bring on themselves due to their disobedience. I'm not suggesting that if you are in God's will everything will be rosy. But I am saying that many tragedies can be avoided by simply staying close to God. It would have been foolish for Noah and his family to venture outside the ark after the rain began, thinking they could swim back when the water started rising. Unfortunately, many people play this game of Russian Roulette with their soul. They not only tempt God, but they open the door for the devil to wreak havoc in their lives and then wonder why God let them down. Friend, stay in the ark of safety. Too many dangers lurk outside the fold. I've seen many people leave their church because they got offended over some trivial issue, then calamity struck and before long their lives and/or their families fell apart. We must realize we need each other. We need the fellowship of believers. We need to surround ourselves with like-minded people who will keep us encouraged in the Lord. Just by simply staying in the house, many tragedies can be avoided.

Is the Grass Really Greener?

The Prodigal Son (Lu. 15:11–32) learned how important it is to stay in the house the hard way. After succumbing to the lie that the grass was greener on the other side of the fence, he demanded his inheritance and squandered it on "riotous living." *"And when he had spent all, there arose a famine in the land; and he began to be in want."* Suddenly, his fair-weather friends were gone and he was left out in the cold. You see, eventually the fun of sin (what lures people out of the house to start with) wears off and the consequences of sin start taking their toll. Before his money ran out, the prodigal lived high on the hog. Afterwards, the only job he could find was feeding hogs. He became so hungry he would have eaten the swine feed if allowed. Finally, when he hit rock bottom, *"he came to himself"* and realized his father's slaves were better off than he was. So he worked up the courage to return home. No doubt he rehearsed his apology to his father during his long journey. He expected (and would have welcomed) to be treated like a servant. Instead, his father saw him in the distance and ran to him and kissed and embraced him. His father ordered the servants to bring out the best robe (symbolic of righteousness), a ring (a token of union and authority) and shoes (the badge of sonship and freedom), three items he probably pawned for a few meals. A feast was prepared and the prodigal was restored to all the rights and privileges of sonship.

Late that first night back in his father's house, after all the celebration subsided, I can imagine this wayward son laying down in his old bedroom. The familiar surroundings brought back a rush of fond memories. And as he stared at the ceiling retracing his steps of the past few months, he must have asked himself, "Why did I ever leave?" Restored? Yes! A new beginning? Yes! But look at the scars, the wasted time and resources, the painful memories, the regrets and the repercussions of falling out of fellowship with his father. An ounce of prevention is truly worth a pound of cure. In regard to temptation, the grass is always the greenest near the septic tank. Sin, like a lure, is usually attractive. But lures have hidden hooks. If there was no fun in sin nobody would commit it. The catch is the fun in sin is short-lived. (Heb. 11:25) Herein lies the *"deceitfulness of sin"* (Heb. 3:13); Satan seduces us with the temporary pleasures of sin while craftily concealing the long-term consequences. This young man just wanted to have some fun away from the strict rules of his father's house. He learned the hard lesson that sin takes you farther than you want to stray, keeps you longer than you want to stay and costs you more than you want to pay. It seems I can hear the regretful thoughts of this young man as he looks back in retrospect, "If only I had just stayed in the house!"

Response #2. Become Bitter

When Jesus finally arrived in Bethany four days after Lazarus' death, Mary and Martha were at their wits end. As Jesus approached the town, Martha, who had cooked so many meals for Him and perhaps washed or mended His clothes, ran to meet Him brokenhearted. But Mary, the one who had sat so intently at His feet, *"...Sat still in the house."* (Jn. 11:20 KJV) She was so disappointed, so devastated that she couldn't even face Jesus at first. The following statement is not an indictment on any modern woman who bears the name Mary, but, in Bible times, the name Mary meant *"bitter."*[24] (It is related to the name Marah—the place where the Children of Israel discovered undrinkable water. Upon God's instructions, Moses cut down a nearby tree, threw it into the water and, as a result of his obedience, the water was made sweet. This was a type of how the waters of humanity were polluted by sin and how, when Jesus— The Branch—was cut down, He made the water drinkable again (Ex. 15:23-25).

Mary probably resented the lack of response on Jesus' part when she and Martha sent the urgent message concerning their brother's illness. No doubt they had come to expect special favors of the Master considering all they had done for His ministry and for Him personally. The Gospels describe the special relationship Jesus shared with this family. A special relationship should entitle them to special favors, right? Dr. James Dobson makes a thought-provoking observation in his excellent book *When God Doesn't Make Sense.* Why was Jesus out somewhere preaching to total strangers when His personal friends, His second family practically, was in dire need?[25] Mary's faith was wounded. She probably thought that God had let her down. He didn't come through when she needed Him the most.

Then Jesus sent Martha back to their house to get Mary (Jn. 11:28). The sisters hurried back to meet Him. John tells how the story unfolds, *"When Mary reached the place where Jesus was and saw Him, she fell at His feet and said, 'Lord, if You had been here, my brother would not have died.'"* (Jn. 11:32 NIV) She quotes verbatim the sentiments of Martha recorded in verse 21. These sisters simply could not understand how anything was more important to Jesus than their sick brother. Have you ever felt that way? Have you ever felt like God was putting you off or ignoring you because there was no immediate response to your desperate plea? Friend, you are not alone. I suppose every Christian will feel that way at some point.

The Root of Bitterness

Martha blamed Jesus verbally. Mary, the less vocal of the two, blamed Jesus too but in a more subtle way. She became bitter—she turned her disappointment and anger inward. Bitterness manifests in resentment and usually results from any one of the following: grief, disappointment, abuse, mistreatment, injustice, failure, broken promises, unanswered prayers, frustration, etc. Bitterness is something that festers inside like a cancer and will destroy a person spiritually if they don't deal with it. Bitter people tend to be overly skeptical, cynical, pessimistic, distrusting, suspicious of others and even spiteful. In fact, the word bitter is closely related to the word bite and originally meant *"biting, cutting, cruel."*[26] The Bible warns us strongly about this poison of the soul with these words: *"Looking diligently lest any man fail of the grace of God; lest any **root of bitterness** springing up trouble you, and thereby many be defiled...."* (Heb. 12:15 KJV) I've met some disenchanted wives who were so mistreated by their husbands that they harbored a subconscious animosity for men in general. The wounds were so deep, the bitterness manifested in mean-spirited comments to total strangers. I've also encountered many young people who resented their parents maliciously due to repeated broken promises. I'm sure you know individuals who have had more than their share of misfortune and now they view lifc and othcr pcople through the dark lenses of their painful personal experiences.

Again, I believe many people are out of church today due to this very thing. Others who wouldn't dare quit attending church altogether, are just going through the motions of outward religion but they are dying inside from the poison of bitterness that has defiled their spirit. Some of this we bring on ourselves. Sometimes we believe in an illusion and when the illusion proves untrue, we become disillusioned and bitter.

When I was about twelve, I did one of the most bone-headed things of my entire life. I had saved up about forty dollars by mowing a few lawns in the neighborhood. We lived on a lake in Florida and always had a boat or two, but I wanted to have my very own two-man, inflatable raft. When I brought it home from the store, a friend and I pumped it up and carried it down to the lake for its maiden voyage. We took along some fireworks for kicks. We paddled out a hundred yards or so from shore and started setting off the fireworks. We lit the firecrackers and threw them overboard only miliseconds before the fuses burned down and they exploded. All was going fine until we got to the bottle rockets. We forgot to bring a bottle along. So, without thinking, we propped one against the side of the rubber raft and lit it. As soon as the fuse ignited, sparks went flying. Everywhere a spark landed it sizzled a hole in my brand new raft I'd worked so hard to purchase. As the air escaped, the raft deflated rapidly. We started paddling frantically toward the shore but the raft was already taking in water. Fortunately, we were both good swimmers and the water wasn't all that deep. We just took an unexpected swim fully clothed.

The point to this silly story is that some believers have adopted beliefs (rafts) that are un-seaworthy. They float along fine until adversity (the fireworks of life) strikes and punctures holes in the soft underbelly of their theology. All of a sudden, the things they never believed could happen to a Christian, much less them, causes their faith to capsize and they are left flailing in the water, trying desperately to stay afloat. Because many Christians believe the unscriptural illusion that tragedy can never happen to them, they are so shell-shocked if it does that they become disillusioned (their faith is wounded). This leads to either blaming God who, in their minds, let them down or being bitter about matters of faith because what they believed proved to be untrue.

A Tale of Three Widows

A Biblical example of how tragedy can drive a person into bitterness can be found in the first chapter of Ruth. Elimelech and Naomi, a Jewish couple, moved from Bethlehem to Moab with their two sons during a famine. Not long after they arrived, Elimelech died. Naomi's two sons, Mahlon and Chilion, married two women from Moab, named Orpah and Ruth. Another ten years drifted by and both of Naomi's sons died also, leaving the three widows in a quandary about what to do next. Naomi decided she'd had enough of Moab and determined to return to the land of Israel, *"For she had heard in the country of Moab that the Lord had visited His people by giving them bread."* (Ru. 1:6) In other words, the famine was over. Naomi pled with her daughters-in-law to remain in Moab because she didn't have any means to support them, much less a promising future to offer them. While Orpah kissed Naomi goodbye, Ruth clung to her and uttered one of the most inspiring passages in the entire Bible. In fact, her reply is still used today for vows in many wedding ceremonies (Ru. 1:16–17). When Naomi and Ruth returned to Bethlehem, none of Naomi's friends recognized her (Ru. 1:19). The following passage was spoken out of such deep grief and bitter disappointment, you can actually feel the wounded faith of this broken woman: *"...Don't call me Naomi... [pleasant]*[27] *call me Mara [bitter]*[28]*, because the Almighty has made my life very **bitter**. I went away full, but the Lord has brought me back empty. Why call me Naomi? The Lord has afflicted me; the Almighty has brought misfortune upon me."* (Ru. 1:20–21 NIV)

On the surface, this story seems innocuous enough, but careful study reveals pertinent lessons pertaining to our subject. First of all, they lived in Bethlehem. Bethlehem means *"House of Bread"*[29] and is a fitting type of the Church or being in the will of God. The church is supposed to be the house of bread that nourishes the needs of starving humanity. (Thus it was significant and appropriate for Jesus to be born in Bethlehem because He was "The Bread of Life.")

Secondly, they moved to Moab. Moab means *"waste"* or *"nothingness"*[30] and, though it was only about thirty miles from Bethlehem, it was a heathen culture. The Moabites worshiped an idol named Chemosh to which child and human sacrifice was commonplace. Moab was named after the son of Lot. This child was born of an incestuous relationship Lot had with his daughter as he fled from God's wrath on Sodom and Gomorrah (Gen. 19: 30–37). Moab is, therefore, a dark type of evil, the sinful world and getting out of the will of God.

So what we have here is a picture of a family making a disastrous decision to leave the land of Israel, where the inhabitants tended to worship the one, true God for a land of idolatry. To modernize this story, we figuratively have a family that is backsliding and leaving the church.

Thirdly, the reason they moved to Moab is noteworthy—there was a famine in the land (Ru. 1:1). Famines, especially in Bible times, were an indication of God's displeasure and chastisement. Instead of skipping town for Moab, Naomi and her husband, along with their fellow citizens, should have repented and asked God to lift the scourge in Bethlehem and plenty probably would have been restored to their land. Rather, they chose to chase the greener grass in Moab and with devastating results—Naomi's husband died and, within ten years, both of her sons died also. Had they taken the time to consider the consequences of getting out of God's will, I'm convinced they would have never left Bethlehem.

Decisions either move us closer to or take us farther away from God.

After burying her two sons, Naomi decided it was time to return home. Decisions usually either move us closer to or take us farther away from God. Before making major decisions, we certainly need to count the cost by asking, "How will this decision affect my relationship with God or the spiritual welfare of my family?" In Naomi's case, it was a poor decision that got her out of God's will. Unfortunately, instead of being thankful that God returned her home at all, she was bitter that the *"**Lord** [had] brought [her] back empty"* (without her husband and two sons). She told all of her old friends, who hardly recognized her, to call her Mara (meaning "bitter")—*"For the Almighty has made my life very **bitter**."* The first chapter of Ruth gives us this portrait of three widows:

1. Naomi—The Grieving Widow. When things went wrong she turned bitter, blamed God and changed her name to indicate her grief. Sadly, many people respond to tragedy in this fashion.

2. Orpah—The Leaving Widow. Orpah hardly hesitated to return to Moab, its way of life and its idolatry. Many people simply try to run from their problems, assuming that by changing their circumstances they can eliminate their troubles.

3. Ruth—The Cleaving Widow. Instead of turning bitter or running from her problems, Ruth clung more tightly to the person she loved. This, no doubt, enabled her to cope with loss of her husband and build a new life.

The good news, of course, is that God brought redemption to Naomi and Ruth through their kinsman, Boaz. Ruth, in fact, became the great grandmother of King David and was one of four Gentile women included in the lineage of Jesus (Rahab, Tamar and Bathsheba being the other three—Mt. 1:1–6). The point, again, is that God can bring good out of bad.

These same three options—**grieving, leaving,** or **cleaving**—present themselves to every one of us when things go wrong. Whether it applies to our marriage, family, job, church or our personal relationship with God. When things turn sour in any of these arenas of life, we can either **grieve** (turn bitter), **leave** (run from our troubles to what we think are greener pastures) or **cleave** (hold on more tightly to those we love and what we know is right and ride out the storm). If we choose the path of Ruth, we will be rewarded both in this life and the next. This leads us to the final and proper response to tragedy.

Response #3. Simply Believe

Back in Bethany in the aftermath of Lazarus' death, Martha tearfully complained to Jesus, *"Lord...if You had been here, my brother would not have died."* Martha implied that if Jesus had only come sooner, before the sickness advanced too far, He could have done something—**yesterday faith**. Jesus responded emphatically, *"Your brother shall rise again."* (Jn. 11:23 NIV) To which Martha replied, *"...I know that he shall rise again in the resurrection **at the last day**."* With this comment Martha affirmed her belief that her brother would be resurrected with all believers at the end of time—**tomorrow faith**. But she didn't have much faith that God could do something in the present. Jesus continued, *"...I am the resurrection and the life. He who believes in Me will live, even though he dies; and whoever lives and believes in Me will never die. **Do you believe this?**"* (Jn. 11:25–26 NIV)

Pay close attention to Martha's answer, *"Yes, Lord...I believe that you are the Christ, the Son of God, who was to come into the world."* Sounds like a pretty good answer but it wasn't what Jesus asked her. He asked, "Do you believe **I am** the resurrection and the life?" In other words, "Do you believe I can do something about this now?" God is the great **I AM**—present tense. He is not just the God of the past or the God of the future; He is the God of the right now! Jesus desired that Mary and Martha simply believe in Him. No doubt, they had seen Him perform many miracles. Instead, they blamed Him and turned bitter until Jesus raised Lazarus from the dead and turned their tears into joy. Jesus simply wanted them to believe even though they did not understand how He could let something like this happen to them.

What do you do when there are no satisfying answers? When there are no clear-cut reasons why? When all the theological explanations are rendered empty and meaningless? When your Lazarus doesn't come back? When your prayers go unanswered and you question God? When your faith is wounded and you feel betrayed? When circumstances come caving in on top of you causing you to doubt everything you've ever believed? What do you do then? The only option to take, when circumstances spin out of our ability to control or comprehend, is to anchor our faith solidly in the Rock of Ages. Just keep believing anyway! Job's life was reduced to a heap of ashes and no one could explain why God allowed it. Job, out of the deepest anguish of the soul, uttered this inspiring phrase, *"Though* [God] *slay me, yet will I trust in Him...."* (Jb. 13:15 KJV) That's what we have to be willing to say and do when life starts spinning out of control. "Lord, I may not understand this, I don't know why You're allowing this to happen to me, it doesn't even make sense, but I will trust You fully anyhow. I will continue to believe in You even when I can't figure everything out. Even when things defy logic and reason, my trust is not in my limited comprehension of theology, my trust is in *You* alone."

Can you imagine what went through Joseph's mind as he walked in that Midianite caravan to Egypt as a slave. Perhaps he questioned the dreams God gave him. Maybe he wondered if he had misinterpreted them. The same brothers who, according to his dreams, were supposed to bow down to him, betrayed him and sold him for the price of a slave. The bottom had fallen out. Everything was topsy-turvy from what he anticipated. Nothing made sense. Then, after being falsely accused of attempted rape by Potiphar's wife, he was sent to prison. It would have been easy for him to lose faith then. He must have wondered, "God, why are you letting this happen to me?" But he never lost faith. He never quit believing. In God's time, some thirteen years after his arrival in Egypt, God vindicated him and took him from pit to pinnacle in one day. As he looked back at all the lonely nights in a dark dungeon, he shared this insight with his brothers some twenty-two years after they betrayed him, *"... Ye thought evil against me; but God meant it unto good...."* (Gen. 50:20 KJV) For sure, as Joseph learned, not everything that happens to us will be good. But God can turn it around and make it work out for our good if we just keep believing.

In 1860, a huge crowd gathered to watch the famous tightrope walker, Blondin, cross the Niagara Falls. He crossed the thousand foot span one hundred and sixty feet above the raging waters numerous times. Amazingly, he not only walked across; he also pushed a wheelbarrow across the vast expanse. One particular boy stared in total disbelief. Blondin noticed the little boy and asked him, "Do you believe I could take a person across in the wheelbarrow without falling?" The boy replied, "Yes, sir. I really do!" Blondin said, "Well then, get in, Son."[31] Therein lies the difference between mere faith and total trust.

Many people claim to "believe" in God. Big deal, so does the devil (Ja. 2:19). But how many are willing to trust Him completely, even when things happen that they think He should prevent?

My parents survived a traumatic experience in the fledgling days of our family. At the time they had two small children, Cindy and Kenny, and my mom was pregnant with their third. This was ten years before I came along and well before the days of sonograms and high-tech medicine. When my mom delivered her baby boy, a severe birth defect was detected—Kerry was born with a hole in his little heart. Back then (late 1950's) there wasn't much doctors could do for him. Two days later, Kerry died. My parents were devastated. How do you cope with the unexplain-able loss of an infant you've carried to full term? After all, my parents were born-again, God-fearing, church-going, tithe-paying believers. That should count for something shouldn't it? How could such a thing happen to them? Grasping for answers, they refused to blame God and turn bitter. Instead, they turned the inner struggle over to God and resolved to trust in His infinite wisdom, even though they didn't pretend to fathom it. In time, with lots of prayer and grace, they got back on their feet again. They would tell you today that it was a time of tre-mendous growth for them spiritually because God brought them through something they never thought they would have to face. In the end, they emerged stronger in their faith, more determined than ever to serve Him.

> *A delay does not necessarily mean a denial.*

God's Character Revealed

It's impossible to know some of the aspects of God's character until you get to a place where you need them. For instance, you can't fully understand how God can comfort you until you face a time of grief in which you need comfort. Likewise you'll never know how He can deliver you from fear until you face fear. Simply put, you will never know how He can be "The Lily of the Valleys" until you find yourself in a valley (Song. 2:1). Remember, the three Hebrew children only encountered "The Fourth Man" when they were thrown into the fire, not before or after, as far as we know (Dan. 3:25). Furthermore, in order to experience God's healing, we may go through times of sickness. I'm convinced that many of the things we face in life are designed as opportunities for God to reveal and manifest His divine attributes. Otherwise, how would we learn what the various facets of His character are? As someone once said, you can't have a testimony without first having a test!

In His Time

Why is God so slow? Have you ever asked that question? Sure you have. Millions of other people have too. My mother likes to say, "God passes up a lot of opportunities to be early." Maybe He's seldom early, but God is never late either. As many Christian songs remind us, He's an on-time God. However, that doesn't always seem to be the case because there is a huge disparity between our time and His. After all, Jesus said, *"Behold, I come quickly...."* (Rev. 22:12) and that was 2,000 years ago. So, obviously, His "quickly" and our "quickly" don't mean exactly the same thing. Then again, we have to keep in mind that *"...One day is with the Lord as a thousand years, and a thousand years as one day."* (2 Pt. 3:8 KJV)

Another factor to consider is that we live in such a fast-paced society. We are accustomed to getting things we want instantly. With the advent of drive through service, 1-hour photo, microwave ovens, electronic mail, instant credit, ATM's, etc., we have become conditioned to getting what we ask for at the push of a button, the click of a mouse or the swipe of a credit card. All of this fosters a certain sort of impatience. If we are not careful, our demand for immediate responses can carry over into our prayer lives. Make no mistake, there are no shortcuts to walking with and waiting on God. The Bible says:

"Be still, and know that I am God." (Ps. 46:10 KJV)

"...He who comes to God must believe that He is, and that He is a rewarder of those who diligently seek Him." (Heb. 11:6)

"But they that wait upon the Lord shall renew their strength...." (Is. 40:31 KJV)

"Wait on the Lord: be of good courage, and He shall strengthen thine heart: wait, I say, on the Lord." (Ps. 27:14 KJV)

If we are not careful, the impatience of our society can creep into our spiritual life and we can miss out on God's blessings because we aren't willing to wait. After all, the apostles had to tarry in the upper room for approximately ten days before they were endued with the power of the Holy Ghost (Lu. 24:49). Remember how Mary and Martha asked why Jesus hadn't come sooner to heal Lazarus? To them, He was late. To Jesus, He was right on time. What about Joseph? It was approximately twenty-two years after he told his brothers his dream about them bowing down to him that it came to pass. I'm sure Joseph thought many times, "God, why is it taking so long?" What about David? He was anointed king by Samuel as a teenager but many years lapsed, while Saul chased him like a fugitive, before he felt the weight of the crown on his head. He probably wondered many times if he would even live long enough to become king? Then there's Abraham. God promised him a son when he was seventy-five years old.

Isaac wasn't born until Abraham was a hundred and Sarah was ninety. Imagine how many times they questioned why God was so slow. Did God derive some kind of pleasure from prolonging their misery? Certainly not! God waited until there was no humanly possible way for them to conceive so that when Isaac was born everyone would know that it was a miracle.

The list goes on and on of the Bible characters who discovered that God's timing was not their timing. You see, God is not bound by our 365 day-per-year calendar. He is not limited to our seven day-per-week schedules or our twenty-four hour days. He is eternal! Our deadlines pose no restriction on Him. He has a higher perspective on everything. That's why we must learn to trust Him even when He seems to be late. While from our perspective it may appear He is late, from His perspective He's not late at all—He's right on time! Remember, a delay does not mean a denial.

Daniel, for instance, fasted and prayed for three weeks regarding a certain matter before the answer came. Finally, an angel revealed to him that *"...From the first day...your words were heard...but the prince of the kingdom of Persia withstood me twenty-one days...."* (Dan. 10:12–13) God heard Daniel's prayer immediately but the angel returning with his answer was detained by the Prince of Persia (apparently a demonic spirit that controlled the Persian Empire) until Michael, the archangel, helped defeat him. So if the answer to your prayer seems delayed, don't assume that God has forgotten you or is ignoring you. There is more going on in the spirit world than we realize. Hang in there and the answer will come. As Solomon so aptly put it, *"He* [makes] *every thing beautiful **in His time**...."* (Ec. 3:11 KJV)

This is not to suggest that God can't or won't work a miracle in your life instantaneously. I personally know many people who have received instantaneous miracles of healing or other acts of divine intervention. Ephesians 3:20 reminds us that God is *"...Able to do exceeding abundantly above all that we ask or think...."* But how and when God moves is entirely up to Him. He is sovereign and He simply wants us to trust Him no matter what.

Overcoming and Enduring Faith

I think it's important to remember that not all hurts will be healed in this life. Not all rewards or all punishments will be administered in this world. But the Bible clearly indicates that there are no wounds inflicted upon us here that heaven can't heal. Part of the faith walk is holding on to the promises of God despite unfavorable circumstances. One day, all of the things that we see as unfair and unjust, God will rectify by settling all accounts. He keeps good records. And in time, He will right every wrong. Meanwhile, we need to realize that the Patriarchs of Faith didn't receive everything they believed for either, but they kept on believing anyhow.

*"These all died in faith, **not having received the promises**, but having seen them afar off were assured of them, embraced them and confessed that they were strangers and pilgrims on the earth. For those who say such things declare plainly that they seek a homeland. But now they desire a better, that is, a heavenly country. Therefore God is not ashamed to be called their God, for He has prepared a city for them."* (Heb. 11:13–14, 16)

Later, the author of Hebrews wrote of both the great victories achieved through faith and the horrific hardships endured by faith (Heb. 11:33–38). Unfortunately, in our shallow, modern definition of faith, many emphasize the overcoming aspect of faith and completely ignore the enduring aspect of faith. God's endorsement of those who believed despite enduring great sorrow was that the world was not even worthy of them (Heb. 11:38). *"And these all, having obtained a good report through faith, received not the promises."* (Heb. 11:39 KJV) So faith is not just the God-given ability to believe and receive, faith is also the God-given ability to continue believing when, for some unknown reason, you don't receive.

It Is Well With My Soul

A great example of someone who continued to believe God despite enduring devastating tragedy was songwriter Horatio Spafford. Born in New York in 1828, Spafford was a Chicago Presbyterian layman who penned the lyrics to the great hymn titled above. Few know that this song was born out of the deepest tragedy imaginable. Spafford became a successful lawyer in Chicago. His prosperity had no affect on his involvement in Christian work. He was a personal friend of the great Evangelist Dwight L. Moody. Spafford attended Moody's meetings and financially supported his and other prominent ministries of that era. Spafford was described by George Stebbins, a noted Gospel musician, as a "man of unusual intelligence and refinement, deeply spiritual, and a devoted student of the Scriptures."

Spafford was no stranger to tragedy. He lost heavy real estate investments in the disastrous Chicago fire of 1871. Additional grief ensued when his only son died. Seeking rest and solace, he and his wife scheduled a vacation in Europe with their four daughters in 1873. They planned their trip to coincide with one of D. L. Moody's revival campaigns in Great Britain. Due to unexpected business, Mr. Spafford remained in Chicago but sent his wife and four girls ahead on the *S. S. Ville du Havre*. He intended to catch another ship to meet them later. On November 22, 1873, the unthinkable happened—the ship his wife and daughters were aboard was struck by an English vessel, the *Lochearn*, and sank in twelve minutes. Despite Mrs. Spafford's desperate efforts to save her daughters, all four drowned. When the survivors were rescued, they were

Mrs. Spafford cabled her husband just two words, "Saved alone."

taken to Cardiff, Wales where they were each allowed a brief telegram. Mrs. Spafford cabled her husband just two words, "Saved alone." Mr. Spafford, having heard about the collision understood what the words meant— his wife was alive, his daughters had perished.

Spafford sailed to meet and grieve with his bereaved wife. No doubt as he stood on the bow of the ship, his emotions churned. Part of him wanted to blame God and demand why. The other part simply wanted to trust God no matter what. During the voyage, Spafford surely relived over and over the unbearable pain of losing all five of his children. Can't you see him pacing the deck wringing his hands and wiping away profuse tears. Staring over the bow into the angry sea, he desperately longed to reach down and reclaim his little ones. I imagine he agonized over the fact that he wasn't with his family when the accident occurred. "Why wasn't I there? What business was so important that I couldn't get away to be with them? Maybe I could have saved them? I could have done something. Why, God, why?"

As the inner war of emotions and unanswered questions raged, a song was born. It is speculated that as Spafford's ship sailed in the general vicinity where his daughters drowned that out of the agony of his soul flowed these words:

> *When peace like a river attendeth my way,*
> *When sorrows like sea billows roll.*
> *Whatever my lot, Thou hast taught me to say,*
> *It is well, it is well with my soul.*

Remarkably, Mr. Spafford didn't dwell on his own bitter sorrows in this song. In the next two verses, notice how he shifts his focus on Christ's suffering and the redemptive work of Calvary.

> *Tho' Satan should buffet, tho' trials should come,*
> *Let this blessed assurance control,*
> *That Christ hath regarded my helpless estate,*
> *And hath shed His own blood for my soul.*

> *My sin, O the bliss of this glorious tho't,*
> *My sin, not in part, but the whole,*
> *Is nailed to the cross and I bear it no more:*
> *Praise the Lord, praise the Lord, O my soul!*

Finally, in the fourth verse, Mr. Spafford turns his attention to the glorious return of Jesus Christ when all wrongs in this life will be made right.

And, Lord, haste the day when my faith shall be sight,
The clouds be rolled back as a scroll:
The trump shall resound and the Lord shall descend,
Even so it is well with my soul.[32]

This man, Horatio Spafford, exemplified the brand of faith you read about in Hebrews eleven. Having faith doesn't always mean you'll get what you want. Having faith means that whether you receive it or not, you still keep believing. Sure it takes faith to believe God for a healing and then see it materialize. But it takes a stronger, more mature faith to believe God for a healing and when it doesn't come to pass, continue believing that God is a healer. It's wonderful and relatively easy to believe *after* we've seen God move (like Thomas Jn. 20:24–28). But what if He doesn't? What if the healing doesn't manifest? What if your prayers remain unanswered? What if your Lazarus doesn't come back from the grave? What will you do then? We all have three main choices, we can (1.) Blame God (2.) Become bitter or (3.) Simply keep believing. Jesus said to Thomas, "*...Because you have seen Me, you have believed. Blessed are those who have not seen and yet have believed.*" (Jn. 20:29)

I am not by any means trying to discourage you from expecting God to answer your prayers and meet your needs. I am simply trying to get you to evaluate the basis for your faith. If it is based on circumstances, your faith will fluctuate with them. If your faith is based on the faithfulness of God, then you won't be shaken despite adverse circumstances. Even when life doesn't seem fair, God is faithful. When God doesn't make sense, He is faithful. When you, like Martha and Mary, wonder why He's so late, He is faithful. When others get healed and you don't, He is still faithful. When your desperate pleas for help seem ignored, He is still faithful. Job must have anchored his faith in the faithfulness of God for him to say, *"...I know that my Redeemer lives...."* (Jb. 19:25) After losing his ten children and most of his wealth, it sure didn't look like his Redeemer was alive or that He was concerned about Job's plight. But Job kept believing anyway and eventually redemption came. *"...The Lord blessed the latter end of Job more than his beginning...."* (Jb. 42:12 KJV) Horatio Spafford must have had this same understanding about God's faithfulness. How else could a man who lost five children write such inspiring words? Nothing else was "well" in his life, but it was "well" with the most important thing in the light of eternity—his soul.

A Peace That Passes Understanding

I want to close with a few comforting thoughts on peace. Philippians 4:7 reads, *"And the peace of God, which surpasses all understanding, will guard your hearts and minds through Christ Jesus."* This passage takes on special significance in the time of tragedy—a time when ordinary people have little or no peace. Panic or fear are more common. But God can give a peace in troubled times to believers that simply mystifies unbelievers. They will look at you and ask, "How can you be so calm? How are you coping with this? What's keeping you from stressing out?" Your answer will be that, "Jehovah Shalom—*The Lord my Peace*—lives in my heart and He's the One enabling me to handle this. He is sustaining me by His grace." Incidentally, the term "Jehovah Shalom" was used by Gideon to name his altar during a time of oppression by the Midianites (Jd. 6:24). So in a time of war, Gideon dared to declare that God was his source of peace. This reminds me of a quote I heard years ago—"Peace is not the absence of conflict; peace is the presence of God in the midst of the conflict!"[33]

Another way to interpret this verse (Ph. 4:7) is that God can give us peace beyond the need for understanding. In fact, the word *peace* in this verse means *"To hold oneself above, to excel, superior, higher."*[34] So God's peace is "superior" and "higher" to understanding and surpasses the need for it. Thus, all the things about the apparent unfairness of life we can relinquish to the Lord. He will grant us a supernatural peace so we won't have to worry about what is beyond our control. Take a moment to do this. Have you been wrestling with unanswered questions? Have you been tempted to blame God for your misfortunes? Has a tragedy struck your life that has left you reeling? Are you fighting bitterness? Have you wondered why God could let something like "this" happen to you? Friend, you are not alone. Many other believers are facing the same doubts, fears and questions. Turn all of these disturbing issues over to the Lord. As the old hymn of the faith recommends, "Take your burdens to the Lord and leave them there." Let the Lord minister peace to your troubled heart. In the aftermath of any tragedy, there is a whirlwind of emotions that can drive us to the brink of despair. But God can whisper

> *"Peace is not the absence of conflict; peace is the presence of God in the midst of the conflict."*

"Peace be still" to the raging storm and He can calm the troubled waters of your soul. Take a moment to "[Cast] *all your care upon Him, for He cares for you."* (1 Pt. 5:7)

Jesus knew that His own death would present an overwhelming tragedy to His followers. Perhaps that is why, in the closing hours of His life, He spoke these reassuring words to them,

Take your burdens to the Lord and leave them there.

"I will not leave you comfortless: I will come to you...Peace I leave with you, my peace I give you: not as the world giveth, give I unto you. Let not your heart be troubled, neither let it be afraid." (Jn. 14:18, 27 KJV)

I trust as a result of reading this book: that your faith has been increased in the supernatural power of God, that you have resolved to trust God no matter what you face in life, that you will resist the temptation to blame God or to turn bitter when things go wrong, that you will turn over to God all the things you don't understand, and, most of all, that you will realize that the God we serve is a God of redemption. He can bring good out of any bad situation! He never promised that everything that happened to us would be good. But He did promise that *"...All things work together for good to those who love God...."* (Ro. 8:28) One day we will all look back on the tragedies that have us so perplexed and realize that there really was a strategy behind tragedy. There was and is meaning to all our suffering. God is aware of our pain and He has been working behind the scenes all along. Like Joseph, our final declaration to the devil should be *"... You thought evil against me;*

but God meant it for good...." (Gen. 50:20) Keep fighting the good fight of faith. God can turn your situation around 180 degrees overnight. He's done it many times before. He'll do it again. He will bring good out of bad for you. God will give you beauty for ashes in His time. So until our answer comes, let us continue practicing the words of Paul, *"And let us not be weary in well doing: for in due season* [in His time] *we shall reap, if we faint not."* (Gal. 6:9 KJV)

A Model for Miracles

If you or someone you know needs a miracle, I encourage you to re-read the suggestions found in chapter five (pages 67–77). In addition, there are some other keys to miracles that I have reserved for this final chapter. There is no ironclad formula that works one hundred percent of the time. No magic wand that manufactures miracles exists. However, by studying and applying Biblical principles we can construct a model that will greatly increase the likelihood of receiving one.

When I was young my mother did a lot of sewing. I can vividly recall going to fabric stores with her to pick out patterns. At home I'd curiously watch her pin a pattern to a piece of material and then carefully cut around it with sharp scissors. She could make any dress, skirt or blouse she wanted by simply following the pattern. The Bible gives us the model for receiving miracles. I believe God is more eager to grant healings than we are to receive them. We can place ourselves in a receptive position by simply following the model outlined in His Word.

A good way to do that is to examine how people received miracles in the Bible and follow their example.

A noted evangelist who had many documented miracles in his ministry was approached by a skeptic who emphatically stated, "I don't believe in miracles!" Unshaken, the minister confidently responded, "When you need a miracle, then you will start believing in them." Friend, when you are faced with a situation in which God is the only source you can look to for help, you are a prime candidate for a miracle.

President Abraham Lincoln, during the dark days of the American Civil War, admitted, *"I have been driven many times to my knees by the overwhelming conviction that I had nowhere else to go."*[35] We would all do well to make God our first resource instead of our last resort. This reminds me of an old familiar hymn:

> *Where could I go?*
> *Where could I go?*
> *Seeking a refuge for my soul,*
> *Needing a friend,*
> *To help me in the end,*
> *Where could I go but to the Lord?*

Realize the Power of Prayer

The vast majority of people who experienced miracles in the Bible employed the power of prayer. John Wallace wrote, *"Prayer moves the hand that moves the world."*[36] Prayer enables us to tap into a supernatural power source when human effort is insufficient. The power of prayer is immeasurable—*"The effective, fervent prayer of a righteous man avails much."* (Ja. 5:16)

It is the key to the heart of God that unlocks all of the resources of heaven. James wrote, *"... You do not have because you do not ask."* (Ja. 4:2) F. B. Myer observed, *"The great tragedy of life is not unanswered prayer, but unoffered prayer."*[37] Another beloved hymn conveys the same message:

> *"O what peace we often forfeit,*
> *O what needless pain we bear,*
> *All because we do not carry,*
> *Everything to God in prayer."*

The Bible is replete with examples of how prayer turned the tide in the favor of God's people:

- The cries of Israel moved God to deliver them from slavery in Egypt. (Ex. 2:23)

- The prayer of Elijah shut up the rains for three and a half years. (Ja. 5:17–18)

- The desperate prayer of Hannah produced a son. (1 Sam. 1:12–20)

- The prayer of Hezekiah added fifteen years to his life. (2 Kgs. 20:1–6)

- Prayer sparked a revival in Nineveh and postponed judgment. (Jo. 3:8–10)

- The New Testament Church was spawned out of a prayer meeting. (Ac. 1:14)

- Prayers of Jesus and the Apostles healed the sick and raised the dead.

- Paul and Silas' prayers sprung them from jail via an earthquake. (Ac. 16:25–26)

Many other examples could be cited. If you are facing an overwhelming crisis, do what the Psalmist David recommended, *"From the end of the earth I will cry to You, when my heart is overwhelmed; lead me to the Rock that is higher than I."* (Ps. 61:2) In other words, when your problem is bigger than you, appeal to the God who is bigger than the problem. Prayer connects you to a supernatural God who can do what no other power can do. Notice in the verse above David wrote, *"I will **cry** to You."* That indicates urgency and desperation. If my children just *call* me I may come at my leisure. But when they *cry*, I come running. So it is with God. Furthermore, Jesus taught there is special power in agreeing in prayer with other believers, *"Again I say to you that **if two of you agree** on earth concerning anything that they ask, it will be done for them by My Father in heaven."* (Mt. 18:19) I strongly recommend that you find someone who will pray with you frequently in agreement until you receive your answer.

Utilize Biblical Methods

There are proven Biblical methods of receiving healing that we need to employ. Keep in mind that God doesn't always heal the same way every time. Also, God can work miracles sovereignly without human assistance. But, more often than not, He chooses to work through people.

Laying on of Hands: One method that Jesus and the Apostles utilized in healing the sick and in imparting spiritual gifts is the laying on of hands. This provides a point of contact and a means of transfer from anointed, faith-filled ministers to a person in need. In a spiritual sense, it is similar to the surge of power one battery receives from another when jumper cables are connected. Surplus energy from a strong battery is essentially transferred to a weak battery by connecting the two. In my case, my pastor, Bertha Madden, laid hands on me and prayed the prayer of faith that resulted in my healing. This pattern of ministry emerges as you study the New Testament:

- *"…He **laid His hands** on a few sick people and healed them."* (Mk. 6:5–6)

- *"When the sun was setting, all those who had any that were sick with various diseases brought them to Him; and He **laid His hands on every one of them** and healed them."* (Lu. 4:40)

- *"And He **laid His hands on her**, and immediately she was made straight…."* (Lu. 13:13)

- *"And these signs will follow those who believe: in My name…they will **lay hands on the sick**, and they will recover."* (Mk. 16:17–18)

- *"Then they **laid hands on them**, and they received the Holy Spirit."* (Ac. 8:17)

- *"Paul went in to him and prayed, and he **laid his hands on him** and healed him."* (Ac. 28:8–9)

- *"Therefore I remind you to stir up the gift of God which is in you through the **laying on of my hands**."* (2 Tim. 1:6)

If you need a miracle, I urge you to seek out anointed, Spirit-filled ministers who believe in the supernatural power of God to lay hands on you and pray the prayer of faith over you. Especially look for those who operate in the gifts of healing, miracles and faith (1 Cor. 12:9–10). It may be the key to your breakthrough.

Anointing With Oil: Another method of healing Jesus and His disciples used is anointing with oil. *"So they went out and preached that people should repent. And they cast out many demons, and **anointed with oil** many who were sick, and healed them."* (Mk. 6:12–13) Oil has no inherent magical qualities, although it was used for medicinal purposes in Bible times (Lu. 10:34). Oil is symbolic of the anointing power of the Holy Spirit. Like the laying on of hands, it represents a point of contact. It is a means by which the dynamic power of the Holy Spirit is released. *"Is anyone among you sick? Let him call for the elders of the church, and let them pray over him, **anointing him with oil** in the name of the Lord. And the prayer of faith will save the sick, and the Lord will raise him up."* (Ja. 5:14–15)

Often a spiritual anointing accompanies a physical anointing. David was anointed with oil by Samuel as a shepherd boy. With that literal anointing came a spiritual endowment that enabled him to defeat Goliath, drive evil spirits away from King Saul with his music and thrive during years of persecution before he assumed the throne of Israel. No wonder David wrote in his most famous psalm, *"You anoint my head with oil...."* (Ps. 23:5) The Prophet Samuel poured oil on David's head, but God poured supernatural power into David's life that resulted in an ordinary man doing extraordinary things.

Anointing with oil is a method God uses in healing the sick and ordaining spiritual leaders.

The Spoken Word: It should be noted that God is not limited to actual physical contact for healing. Jesus performed some miracles by merely speaking the word and the effects were manifested miles away. There is no distance in prayer. Jesus healed both the Centurion's servant (Mt. 8:5–13) and the Nobleman's son (Jn. 4:46–53) in this fashion. The Centurion knew the power of words. As a captain he ordered hundreds of soldiers into battle by simply issuing verbal commands. He asked Jesus to *"Speak the word only and my servant shall be healed."* Jesus commended his faith and performed the miracle without any physical contact with his sick servant.

The Nobleman came to Jesus in Cana of Galilee from Capernaum, some twenty miles away. Jesus simply said, *"Go your way; your son lives."* (Jn. 4:50) When he returned home, he was informed that his son's fever broke at the precise time Jesus spoke the healing word. If God created the universe by speaking it into existence, He can surely speak through His ministers healing into your body. *"He sent His word and healed them...."* (Ps. 107:20)

Jesus calmed the raging Sea of Galilee by speaking three simple words—*"Peace be still."* (Mk. 4:39) He raised Lazarus from the dead with a short command—*"Lazarus, come forth."* (Jn. 11:43) He healed a deaf and dumb man by uttering the statement—*"Be opened."* (Mk. 7:34) When Jesus delivered Legion from the demonic forces that had him bound, all he said was one word—*"Go."* (Mt. 8:32) You get the idea. There is incredible power in words that are spoken in faith and under the anointing. Proverbs 18:21 declares, *"Death and life are in the power of the tongue."* No wonder Peter cautioned, *"If anyone speaks, let him speak as the **oracles of God**."* (1 Pt. 4:11) An *oracle* is an utterance of God. We are His mouthpiece and spokesmen. In other words, God can anoint our words and speak through us. We can speak victory or defeat into our lives with our words. Use the power of the spoken word to proclaim healing and health over your body.

Fasting: Yet another Biblical method of activating the supernatural is fasting. When the disciples could not cast out a demon and wondered why, Jesus rebuked them for their unbelief. Then He added, *"This kind can come out by nothing but **prayer and fasting**."* (Mk. 9:29) Fasting is a voluntary abstinence from food for the spiritual purpose of drawing closer to God. Fasting is an important Christian discipline. Jesus said, *"**When** you fast..."* (Mt. 6:16), indicating that fasting should be a regular part of our spiritual regimen. The purpose of fasting is not to impress people (Mt. 6:16–18) nor to earn something from God. Rather, fasting denies the flesh and helps us move into a spiritually receptive position. Furthermore, fasting demonstrates to God how serious we are about making spiritual progress. In many instances in the Bible fasting was a deciding factor that triggered a move of God.

Exercise Your Faith

Faith is vital to our salvation and spiritual progress—*"But **without faith** it is impossible to please Him, for he who comes to God **must believe** that He is, and*

that He is a rewarder of those who diligently seek Him."
(Heb. 11:6) Everything we receive from God is obtained
and maintained through faith, including healing and
miracles. An unknown author said, *"Faith sees the invisible, believes the incredible and receives the impossible!"*[38]

Unbelief handcuffs God. That may sound like an
overstatement, but the Bible proves it. In His home town
of Nazareth, Jesus' ministry was hindered due to doubt.
*"**He could do no mighty work there**…and He marveled
because of their **unbelief**."* (Mk. 6:5–6) The Children of
Israel missed out on so many of God's promises and
provisions because they refused to believe:

> *"How often they provoked Him in the wilderness,*
> *And grieved Him in the desert!*
> *Yes, again and again they tempted God,*
> *And **limited the Holy One of Israel**.*
> *They did not remember His power…."*
> (Ps. 78:40–42)

Scripture informs us that "God has dealt to each
one a **measure of faith**." (Ro. 12:3–4) It doesn't specify
how large or small that "measure" is, but God has given
us a certain capacity to believe in Him. There are three
primary ways to increase your faith:

1. Use your faith: When the disciples requested,
"Lord, increase our faith" (Lu. 17:5), Jesus responded, *"If
you have **faith as a mustard seed**, you can say to this
mulberry tree, 'Be pulled up by the roots and be planted in
the sea,' and it would obey you."* (Lu. 17:6) In other words,
it doesn't require a lot of faith to do something great for
God. Just use the faith you have and, like a mustard seed
planted in the soil, it will grow rapidly. If faith is

exercised, like a muscle, it grows stronger. If unused, faith will weaken and fail.

2. Hear the Word: Paul wrote to the Romans, *"So then faith comes by hearing, and hearing by the word of God."* (Ro. 10:17) The more we feed our heart and mind a steady diet of the God's Word, the greater capacity we will have to believe that what God has done for others, He can and will do for us.

3. Fellowship with believers: Faith breeds faith. If you associate with true believers, their spirit will be contagious. Notice how God teamed people together to achieve His purposes. Joshua and Caleb believed the promises of God when an entire generation accepted an evil report of unbelief. Peter and John were a powerful tandem in the Book of Acts. Paul and Barnabus, then later Paul and Silas, were dynamic duos who operated in the supernatural. Fellowshiping with faith-filled people will help you develop your own faith.

Faith is a catalyst (sparkplug) that activates the Word of God and brings the unseen into reality. Faith *"...calls those things which do not exist as though they did."* (Ro. 4:17) Sometimes we have to be headstrong in faith, stubbornly refusing to accept negativism. We must believe it *is* God's will to heal us. Paul instructed Timothy to, *"**Fight** the good fight of faith...."* (1 Tim. 6:12) That involves believing in the healing promises of God despite our feelings, medical reports, or symptoms of sickness. It means believing even when we don't see evidence of our prayers being answered. Remember, a delay does not necessarily mean a denial. In the words of Saint Augustine, *"Faith is to believe what we do not see, and the reward of faith is to see what we believe."*[39]

You might say that faith is the frequency of God. Just as a radio must be tuned to the correct frequency to receive an invisible signal of radio waves, faith tunes us in to the spiritual realm, allowing us to perceive and receive God's promises. Through all of life's peaks and valleys we are reminded to *"walk by faith, not by sight."* (2 Cor. 5:7)

Be prepared for your faith to be tested. The most valuable and strongest metals are refined in the hottest fires. *"That the genuineness of your faith, being much more precious than gold that perishes, though it is **tested by fire**, may be found to praise, honor, and glory at the revelation of Jesus Christ."* (1 Pt. 1:7) Abraham's faith was tested when God required him to offer his son Isaac on the altar (Heb. 11:17–19). God often tests our faith by allowing us to face impossibilities. Before Jesus fed the multitude, He asked Philip where they could buy bread to feed so many. *"But this He said **to test him**, for He Himself knew what He would do."* (Jn. 6:6) Jesus already had a plan in place but He wanted Philip to trust Him for supernatural provision. A person whose faith has been tested knows to do the possible (faith without works is dead) and to rely on God to do the impossible.

Scrutinize Your Life

There are many things that can hinder a healing from manifesting. Taking time for self-examination can reveal barriers to our breakthrough. Bitterness, unforgiveness and unbelief are common barriers to receiving from God. Peter cautioned that mistreating other people can be a cause of unanswered prayers (1 Pt. 3:7).

Unconfessed sin can also interrupt our line of communication with God, *"If I regard iniquity in my heart, the Lord will not hear me."* (Ps. 66:18 KJV) Some things are obviously counterproductive like smoking, drinking, drug use and unhealthy eating habits and actually contribute to the cause of health problems we may pray for God to heal. It's unrealistic to expect God to heal us if we aren't cooperating with the process by walking in the light of known truth.

If you have been seeking for healing and there seems to be a barrier, ask the Holy Spirit to reveal to you what it is. Repent of, renounce and remove from your life anything that grieves God. Be reconciled to people you might be harboring grudges against. Take inventory of your heart and make sure your attitudes, motives and desires are in alignment with God's Word.

You don't have to beg a river to flow, just remove any obstructions. Likewise, you don't have to plead with God to do something He already desires to do for you. Simply remove any hindrances and move into a receptive position. You can do this by looking into the Word and following God's model for miracles.

It is no Secret what God Can Do

Friend, we serve a miracle-working God. He is sovereign, omnipotent (all powerful), omniscient (all knowing) and omnipresent (everywhere). He loves you and has your best interest at heart. Trust Him. Call on His name. Be bold and aggressive in believing. In the words of William Carey, *"Attempt great things for God and expect great things from God."* God specializes in impossible situations and He can do what no other power can do.

In 1949, Billy Graham held a crusade in Los Angeles that vaulted him to national prominence. During the revival, he met an actor named Stuart Hamblen, a hard-drinking star of country western movies and host of a popular radio show. He was notorious for his gambling and brawling. Though the actor attended some of the meetings, he remained unconvinced and unchanged by the Gospel. Near the end of the revival, he called Billy Graham's hotel room at four-thirty in the morning. He asked to meet with the preacher immediately. Under heavy conviction and in tears, the actor gave his heart to Christ on the spot.

The next few days the actor shared his conversion experience on his radio show. Local newspapers picked up the story and promoted the crusade services. Soon all of Los Angeles was buzzing with excitement about the meetings and how God was moving. "The resulting publicity launched a half-century of mass evangelism virtually unparalleled in Christian history."

Sometime later Stuart Hamblen reportedly met movie star John Wayne. The famous cowboy actor asked Hamblen about his conversion. "Well, Duke, it's no secret what God can do." John Wayne thought about that statement for a moment and said, "that sounds like a song." Stuart Hamblen went home, sat down at his piano and wrote these lyrics:

> *"It is no secret what God can do.*
> *What He's done for others, He'll do for you.*
> *With arms wide open, He'll pardon you.*

It is no secret what God can do!"[40]

I can't think of a more fitting way to end this book than to repeat those powerful words—"What He's done for others, He'll do for you!"

The Photo
Review

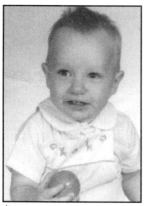

🔼 *It's A Boy:* This picture was taken in 1971, when I was about eighteen months old.

🔼 *A New Addition:* Leslie & Sylvia Godwin (Mom and Dad) are surrounded by Cindy, Kenny, Joel and Jesse (oldest to youngest). The baby is me.

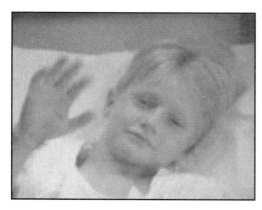

◀ *St. Joseph's Hospital:* I was born in this hospital on August 18, 1969. Not quite eight years later, I returned via the Emergency Room and was admitted for eighteen days to be treated for the leg injuries sustained during my accident. This photo was taken from an 8mm home video.

Home Sweet Home: After eighteen days in the hospital, I was thrilled to be back home. Here I am pictured in our front yard. This photo was also taken from an 8mm video, thus the distortion. My cast was heavy, hot and very itchy in the Florida heat. ➡

Leisure Suit Heaven: *The Godwin family photo (1976), a year before my accident. My mom was expecting my sister Janna at the time. My parents, my sister Cindy, my brothers, Kenny, Joel, Jesse (tallest to shortest), and me. I was the baby until Janna stole my coveted title.*

◄

Little Preacher Boy: *My parents and pastor sensed God's call on my life to preach at that time. I was unaware of it until I turned thirteen in the summer of 1983, when I preached my first sermon.* ▼

↑ **Making A Joyful Noise:** *My brother Kenny taught me how to play the drums. At age 8, I started playing them in our church in Tampa. My ministry started with drumming and I tell people preaching and drums are similar—if you don't know what you are doing, do it louder!*

Faith Pool: *This photo of my parents, Sister Bertha Madden and me was taken shortly after my miracle at her home, where the Faith Pool Prayer Group meetings were held.* ➡

⬆ ***My Parents:*** *Leslie & Sylvia Godwin celebrated 55 years of marriage in January, 2008.*

⬆ ***School Days:*** *I graduated from Gospel Assembly Christian School in May of 1987. Two days later, I went on the evangelistic field to work with, and train under, Evangelist Mike Shreve.*

⬅ ***Taking A Dip:*** *I was five or six in this photo. This was in our backyard, near the spot where my dad baptized me. My brothers, sisters and I grew up swimming, water skiing, boating and fishing on the Big Bay Lake.*

Bread For Children: *In 1989, my testimony was published in "Bread For Children." It was translated into Spanish and sent to many foreign countries. My testimony has been featured in several other publications.* ➡

◀ **Missions:** *In 1988 and 1990, I traveled with Mike Shreve and a team of ministers to Costa Rica. We held open-air crusades, preached in churches and did street evangelism. I was preaching through an interpreter in a Spanish-speaking church. God blessed us with many souls and we witnessed several miracles.*

The Sawdust Trail: *The Gospel tent that I helped Mike Shreve set up in many cities in the 1980's. We usually conducted three-week crusades at each location. This tent measured 160 ft. x 80 ft., and took three days to set up.* ➡

◀ **To Russia With Love:** *In 1999, I accompanied my brother-in-law, Keith Morris, to Tomsk, Siberia, on a mission trip. He and my sister, Cindy, pioneered and pastored a church there. We preached in that church and in several home groups. It was an incredible experience to declare the Gospel in a former communist country and see believers worshipping God freely.*

⬆ Canada: *This photo was taken in the TV studio of 100 Huntley Street, a Canadian network. I've been blessed to share my testimony in hundreds of churches, schools and on many radio and TV programs including LESEA LIVE (Lester Sumrall's TV program) and in R.W. Shambach's 5,000-seat tent in New York.*

⬆ Wedding Bells: *The happiest day of my life was December 11, 1992, when I had the privilege of marrying my true love, Michelle. She is the greatest gift God has given me, second only to my salvation.*

⬅Mike Shreve: *Mike Shreve has imparted many spiritual gifts and much wisdom into my life. He has been my mentor and spiritual father. He has given me opportunities in ministry that one could only dream of. Mike and his wife, Elizabeth, have an international ministry based in Cleveland, Tennessee.*

Original Booklet: *I originally wrote my testimony in booklet form in 1988. God provided the funds to print 3,000 copies of the book. An unknown woman in Illinois came to me in a meeting, handed me an envelope and said, "God told me to give this to you." Inside was a diamond ring that appraised for $3,000—the amount needed to print my book. The cover art illustrates what my leg looked like in the cast I wore. It also depicts my pastor's hands being laid on my leg in the prayer meeting in which I was healed.*

➡

A NEW BONE FOR BEN

A Factual Account of a Creative Miracle

BEN GODWIN

← *The Caboose: My baby sister Janna, who is not pictured in any of the previous photos, replaced me as the caboose on the Godwin family train. This photo was taken a few months prior to my accident.*

↑ **Meet Our Family:** *Ben and Michelle surrounded by their children, Nathan (13), Emily (9) and Noah (2).*

· **T** 7-20-77 IV   **O P E R A T I V E   R E C O R D**   GODWIN, BENJAMIN
                  St. Joseph's Hospital   253877   Rm828

DATE·   7-17-77   SURGEON **R. J. MILLER, M. D.**

PREOPERATIVE DIAGNOSIS: Fracture, acute, traumatic, displaced, compound tibia and fibula left.

POSTOPERATIVE DIAGNOSIS: Same.

OPERATION PERFORMED: Debriement of compound wound of left lower leg with insertion of Steinmann pins and application of long leg cast.

FINDINGS and DESCRIPTION OF OPERATION:

Under satisfactory general anesthesia, the left leg was sterilly prepared and draped. The inspection of the leg revealed an absence of approximately 3 in. of midshaft of tibia and a gaping wound measuring approximately 6 in. in length over the midshaft of the tibia over the medial side of the leg. There were lesser puncture wounds present laterally and medially. The main wound was irrigated and devitalized muscle, dirt and subcutaneous fat were excised. The wound was thoroughly irrigated with approximately 2000 cc of saline. The bone ends were trimmed of dirty material but very little bone was removed. There had been previous loss of considerable amount of bone, approximately 3 inches. The wound was allowed to fall together. No sutures were used except for the ligatures of bleeding points. Adaptic was placed over the exposed muscle. The fascia of the gastroc was incised. The two Steinmann pins were driven across the tibia, both proximally and distally to the fracture site and traction was applied to the leg and a long leg cast applied. The patient was sent to the recovery room in satisfactory condition. Complications: None.

The plan is to return the patient to the OR and do a secondary closure of this wound in a few days if infection does not insue.

D 7-17-77   R. J. MILLER, M. D./ch

OPERATIVE RECORD
13 10/86

O P E R A T I V E   R E C O R D
St. Joseph's Hospital

GODWIN, BENJAMIN   828
No. 253877-4

DATE: **July 22, 1977**   SURGEON: **Richard Miller, M. D.**

PREOPERATIVE DIAGNOSIS: **Healing soft tissue wound with compound fracture of the left tibia and fibula.**

POSTOPERATIVE DIAGNOSIS: **Same.**

OPERATION PERFORMED: **Delayed primary closure of wound.**

FINDINGS and DESCRIPTION OF OPERATION:

Under satisfactory general anesthesia, operating through the window in the previously applied cast, the wound was dressed and appeared to be remarkably clean. The skin edges were approximated except for a one square inch of loss of skin under which overlying the medial head of the gastrocnemius muscle. This was not grafted.

An adaptor dressing was applied and sterile dressing was applied and the patient was sent to the recovery room in good condition.

. D 7-22-77 Richard Miller, M. D./ab

O P E R A T I V E   R E C O R D
13 10/66

```
   T 8-1-77 V            O P E R A T I V E   R E C O R D    GODWIN, BENJAMIN
                             St. Joseph's Hospital           253877   Rm 828
```

DATE: **7-29-77**   SURGEON: R. J. MILLER, M. D.

PREOPERATIVE DIAGNOSIS: Granulating wound left leg.

POSTOPERATIVE DIAGNOSIS: Same.

OPERATION PERFORMED: Split thickness graft right thigh to left shin.

FINDINGS and DESCRIPTION OF OPERATION:

Under satisfactory general anesthesia the left leg and right hip were sterilly prepared. Operating through a window in the left cast the granulating wound was found to measure approximately 2 in. square. A split thickness graft using the battery operated dermatome was removed from the right thigh. This was sutured in place over the granulating wound. Some of the stainless steel sutures previously inserted were removed. Some additional nylon sutures were placed across the previous wound and the split thickness graft was punctured with numerous slits and sutured in place with nylon. Adaptic dressing was placed on both wounds. A pressure dressing was placed on both wounds and the patient was sent to the recovery room in good condition. Blood loss negligable. Prognosis for wound healing is good. The patient will require further surgery on the bone of the left leg.

D 7-29-77/ R. J. MILLER, M. D./cb

O P E R A T I V E   R E C O R D

GODWIN, BENJAMIN D.
253877

DISCHARGE SUMMARY

ADMITTED: 7-16-77   DISCHARGED: 8-2-77

The patient was admitted to the hospital through the E.R. following an
accident in which he was struck by a car on a bicycle. This resulted
in a compound fracture of the left tibia and fibula with a loss of
approximately 3 inches of the shaft of the tibia.

He underwent immediate debridement. The wound was left open. He was
placed in a long leg cast with pins above and below. Subsequent to this
he was returned to the operating room a few days later and secondary
closure of the wound was obtained. Some of the skin was lost and could
not be approximated so that he then had a split thickness graft to cover
an area approximately 2 square inches over the medial side of the calf.

At the time of discharge there was approximately 1 sq. cm. of bone
exposed in the distal fragment. This will require further treatment.

He was discharged in a long leg cast with the pins above and below. He
will be followed as an out patient, and will have to return for further
surgery. It is planned to do a bone graft following wound closure.

D 8-17-77   RICHARD MILLER, M.D./mb

P A T I E N T GODWIN, BENJAMIN

SUMMARY

St. Joseph's Hospital, Tampa, Florida

96) REV. 4/76

End Notes

1. Michael W. Smith, "Hand of Providence," © 1988 Reunion Records.
2. Quotation was taken from medical records from St. Joseph's Hospital, Tampa, Florida, 1977.
3. Ibid.
4. Ibid.
5. Ibid.
6. *The American Heritage Dictionary* (Boston: Houghton Muffflin Company, 1982), p. 300.
7. Ibid.
8. George Sweeting, *Who Said That?* (Chicago: Moody Press, 1994), p. 364.
9. Oscar C. Eliason, *Got Any Rivers to Cross?,* Tennessee Music and Printing Company, Cleveland, 1951.
10. Herbert Lockyer, *All the Women of the Bible* (Grand Rapids: Zondervan Publishing House), pp. 86-87.
11. Herbert Lockyer, *All the Miracles of the Bible* (Grand Rapids: Zondervan Publishing House, 1961), p. 228.
12. Ibid.
13. Ibid., p. 221.
14. Herbet Lockyer, *All the Men of the Bible* (Grand Rapids: Zondervan Publishing House, 1958), p. 216.
15. Gary Smalley and John Trent, Ph.D., *The Two Sides of Love* (Pomona: Focus on the Family Publishing, 1990), p. 6.
16. 4Him, "Why?", Written by Mark Harris/Don Koch/Dave Clark, ©1991 Benson Records.
17. *Great Value in Disaster*, Chicken Soup for the Soul, p. 235.
18. "Edison" *The Reader's Digest Family Encyclopedia of American History*, Pleasantville, N.Y., p. 374.
19. Albert M. Wells Jr., *Inspiring Quotations* (Nashville: Thomas Nelson Publishers, 1988), p. 206.
20. Jack Cavanaugh, "I'll Be Back," *Reader's Digest* (Feb. 1992), pp. 44-49.
21. R.E. Winsett, *We'll Understand It Better By and By*, Tennessee Music and Printing Company, Cleveland, 1951.
22. Stephen Curtis Chapman, "God is God," © 2001 Sparrow Records.
23. "Ptolemy," *Microsoft Encarta Encyclopedia* on CD-ROM (1994 ed.).
24. Lockyer, *All the Women*, p. 92.
25. Dr. James Dobson, *When God Doesn't Make Sense* (Wheaton: Tyndale House Publishers, Inc., 1993), p. 51.
26. *Family Word Finder* (Pleasantville: The Reader's Digest Association, Inc., 1986), p. 94.
27. Lockyer, *All the Women*, p. 116.
28. Ibid., p. 86.
29. Ibid., p. 117.
30. Ibid.

31. Charles R. Swindoll, *The Tale of the Tardy Oxcart* (Nashville: Thomas Nelson Publishers, 1998), p. 586, quoted from Paul Lee Tan, *Encyclopedia of 7,700 Illustrations.*

32. Kenneth Osbeck, "It Is Well With My Soul," *101 Hymn Stories* (Grand Rapids: Kregel Publications, 1982), p. 127.

33. Wells, *Inspiring Quotations,* p.152.

34. James Strong, *Strong's Concordance Greek Dictionary of the Bible,* (Iowa Falls: Riverside Book & Bible House,), p. 74.

35. George Sweeting, *Who Said That?,* p. 361.

36. Ibid., p. 364

37. Wells, *Inspiring Quotations,* p. 160.

38. Ibid., p. 69.

39. Ibid., p. 67.

40. Robert J. Morgan, *Then Sings My Soul,* (Nashville: Thomas Nelson Publishers, 2003), p. 296.

Other Books Published by

Deeper Revelation Books

Producing sound and edifying teaching materials
for the body of Christ.

Publishing loving presentations of Biblical truth
to followers of other worldviews.

⟫⟫·◇·⟪⟪

See the following six pages

For more information visit www.deeperrevelationbooks.org

In Search of the True Light
An in-depth comparison of over 20 world religions
by Mike Shreve

In 1970 Mike Shreve was a teacher of Kundalini Yoga at four universities, and ran a yoga ashram in Tampa, Florida. After a supernatural encounter with the Lord Jesus Christ, his heart, life and belief system were all dramatically changed. In this book he shares his own personal, spiritual journey and compares the beliefs of over 20 religions in seven basic doctrinal areas (something he terms "the seven pillars of wisdom"). Both commonalities and contradictions are revealed. He also addresses concepts like: reincarnation, karma, monism and pantheism, from a Biblical perspective. This one-of-a-kind book will be a great addition to your library! It is a perfect gift for those who are involved in Far Eastern religions seeking ultimate truth.

ISBN: 978-0-942507-73-7   **—Price 19.99**

"This is a great book to give to a non-Christian searching for the truth."   —Kerby Anderson, Point of View Radio Program

"In Search Of The True Light is a classic...I have not been able to put down this book."
—Pastor Matthew Barnett,
The Dream Center

"An incredible research project..."
—C. Peter Wagner, Founder of
Global Harvest Industries

Above:
A portrait of Mike Shreve as a yoga teacher in 1970 and a present day picture.

www.thetruelight.net

MIKE SHREVE, B.Th.,D.D., has been teaching God's Word since 1971. He is the author of nine books and three Bible studies, the founder of "Deeper Revelation Books," and the visionary behind "The True Light Project," an outreach to followers of non-Christian worldviews.

Raised from the Dead
A True Account
by Richard Madison

After a horrible car accident, Richard Madison was pronounced dead-on-arrival. His family was told three times to make funeral arrangements. God revealed Himself to Richard through an out-of-body experience, and ten weeks later he walked out of a wheelchair. He is now a walking miracle testimony to thousands of people throughout the world that God's love can powerfully restore even the most hopeless lives. This amazing book will build your faith.

ISBN: 978-0-942507-43-0   **—Price: $13.95**

RICHARD MADISON is a full-time evangelist who travels the world to tell the remarkable story of how God raised him from his deathbed and completely delivered him from drugs and alcohol. Richard is a highly sought after speaker with a powerful healing and prophetic ministry. He and his family live in Oakman, Alabama.

www.rickmadison.com

Authentic Enlightenment

The inspirational story of a spiritual seeker
by Vail Carruth

Transcendental Meditation still attracts many seekers to its beliefs and practices. Vail Carruth was one of the "originals", joining this group shortly after its introduction in the U.S. In *Authentic Enlightenment* she candidly explains why she was drawn to TM in the early 60s and how she advanced to the point of becoming a certified teacher.

Referred to as a "scientific relaxation technique," TM seemed to bring some benefits. However, this yoga discipline primarily served to turn Vail inward. Though it calmed the senses and opened her to supernatural experiences, still there was something missing. She finally concluded that these techniques would never be able to fill the emptiness of her heart or satisfy her thirst for God.

Vail's spiritual journey took a new direction when she called on the Name above all names—the Name of JESUS. It was only then that she experienced the reality of the HOLY SPIRIT and the unspeakable joy of GOD'S LOVE. Read her story and you, too, will be guided into transformation and wholeness in your life.

ISBN: 978-0-942507-42-3   **—Price: $15.95**

VAIL CARRUTH holds a BA in Fine Art from the University of California, Berkeley, and studied piano at the San Francisco Conservatory of Music. She is a former teacher of TM who shares her experiences in the movement with diverse audiences. Vail is also an artist, even in the way she paints a picture with her words. Her sole desire is to exalt her Creator and to make Him known to others.

www.living-light.net

Our Glorious Inheritance
The Revelation of the Titles of the Children of God
Volume Three—by Mike Shreve

The "OUR GLORIOUS INHERITANCE" eight volume series explores a powerful and edifying subject in God's Word: the revelation of over 1,000 names and titles God has given His people. Each name gives unique insight into a certain aspect of the total inheritance available to sons and daughters of God. Seeing the revelation of ALL of our names and titles provides the most comprehensive and complete view of our spiritual identity—who we are and what we possess as children of God.

In Volume Three, over 150 wonderful and inspiring names for God's people are explored, including: *the Anointed of the Lord, the Blessed of the Father, Children of the Kingdom, Heirs of the Kingdom, God's Garden, Good Ground, Good Seed, Good Soldiers, the Just, Peacemakers, the Poor in Spirit and Trees of Righteousness*. Get ready for a transformational experience!

ISBN: 978-0-942507-54-6   **—Price: $17.95**

God's Promises for your Children
Prayer Devotional
by Mike Shreve

Parenting can really be challenging—sometimes overwhelming. But GOD is on your side! He has given 64 BIBLICAL PROMISES concerning your children—things He pledges to do for them—if you pray and believe.

Scripture declares He is "the faithful God who keeps covenant and mercy to a thousand generations..." (Dt. 7:9). How amazing! Biblically, a "generation" is probably forty years long. Now multiply that by a thousand. That's how long God promises to hover over your family line to manifest covenant provision and merciful care—all because YOU have made a genuine commitment to love and serve Him. Covenant and mercy—those are just two things God pledges to do for your offspring. There are 62 more promises showcased in this prayer devotional.

If you are a parent looking for hope, looking for encouragement, looking for a way out of the storm, looking for a miracle in your family—this is it! This is a revelation that really has the power to change everything!

ISBN: 978-0-942507-05-78   **—Price 14.99**

⇒•◇•⇐

MIKE SHREVE, B.Th.,D.D., has been teaching God's Word since 1971. He is the author of nine books, three Bible studies, and is the founder of "Deeper Revelation Books." He is greatly blessed with a devoted wife, Elizabeth, who assists him in ministry, and two wonderful children, Zion Seth and Destiny Hope, who are both miracles from God.

Ordering Information

For a listing of other available books please visit our website:

www.deeperrevelationbooks.org
or call: 1-423-478-2843

Wholesalers and retailers should contact Anchor Distributors
or Baker &Taylor Distributors at their respective websites:
www.anchordistributors.com
www.btol.com

Individuals desiring these books should send the amount below,
(be sure to include your complete shipping information with
P.O. Box or street address, etc)

plus $5.00 s/h per book to:

Deeper Revelation Books
P.O. Box 4260
Cleveland, TN 37320-4260

You may also order online:
www.deeperrevelationbooks.org or call: 1-423-478-2843

	QTY	PRICE	AMOUNT
GOD'S PROMISES FOR YOUR CHILDREN		$14.99	
IN SEARCH OF THE TRUE LIGHT		$19.99	
OUR GLORIOUS INHERITANCE (Vol. Three)		$17.95	
AUTHENTIC ENLIGHTENMENT		$15.95	
GOD'S STRATEGY FOR TRAGEDY		$14.99	
RAISED FROM THE DEAD		$13.95	
(Add $5.00 s/h per book)	TOTAL AMOUNT		